A Manager's Guide to Developing Competencies in HR Staff

PHYLLIS G. HARTMAN, SHRM-SCP, SPHR

A Manager's Guide to Developing Competencies in HR Staff

Tips and Tools for Improving Proficiency in Your Reports

Society for Human Resource Management
Alexandria, Virginia
www.shrm.org

Strategic Human Resource Management India
Mumbai, India
www.shrmindia.org

Society for Human Resource Management
Haidian District Beijing, China
www.shrm.org/cn

Society for Human Resource Management, Middle East and Africa Office
Dubai, UAE
www.shrm.org/pages/mena.aspx

SOCIETY FOR HUMAN
RESOURCE MANAGEMENT

This publication is designed to provide accurate and authoritative information regarding the subject matter covered. It is sold with the understanding that neither the publisher nor the author is engaged in rendering legal or other professional service. If legal advice or other expert assistance is required, the services of a competent, licensed professional should be sought. The federal and state laws discussed in this book are subject to frequent revision and interpretation by amendments or judicial revisions that may significantly affect employer or employee rights and obligations. Readers are encouraged to seek legal counsel regarding specific policies and practices in their organizations.

This book is published by the Society for Human Resource Management (SHRM). The interpretations, conclusions, and recommendations in this book are those of the author and do not necessarily represent those of the publisher.

SHRM books and products are available on most online bookstores and through the SHRMStore at www.shrmstore.org.

The Society for Human Resource Management is the world's largest HR professional society, representing 285,000 members in more than 165 countries. For nearly seven decades, the Society has been the leading provider of resources serving the needs of HR professionals and advancing the practice of human resource management. SHRM has more than 575 affiliated chapter within the United States and subsidiary offices in China, India, and United Arab Emirates. Please visit us at www.shrm.org.

Interior & Cover Design	Shirley Raybuck
Manager, Creative Services	James McGinnis
Manager, Book Publishing	Matthew Davis
Vice President, Editorial	Tony Lee

Library of Congress Cataloging-in-Publication Data

Hartman, Phyllis G., 1949- author.

A manager's guide to developing competencies in HR staff: tips and tools for improving proficiency in your reports

Alexandria, Virginia: Society for Human Resource Management, 2017

(pbk.: alk. paper) | ISBN: 978-1-586-44438-9 (epub) | ISBN: 978-1-586-44439-6 (emobi) | (epdf) ISBN: 978-5-864-44379-8

Subjects: LCSH: Personnel directors. | Personnel departments--Employees. | Personnel management.

HF5549 .H339 2017
658.3/1245--dc23

Printed in the United States of America

PB Printing 10 9 8 7 6 5 4 3 2   61.11510 | 17-0257

Dedication

For my family: Chuck, Matt, Emma, and Penny. You are what inspires me to live life. For my friends, colleagues, teachers, mentors, and coaches. You spurred me to grow and learn and teach others what you have taught me.

Table of Contents

Introduction

This book provides an easy-to-use guide for HR managers and small business executives to develop employee proficiency in critical HR competencies. Loaded with tips, techniques, assessments tools, and actual stories of management successes, it takes the mystery out of HR staff development.

The Society for Human Resource Management (SHRM) 2016 *HR Trends Report* highlighted continuing and increasing human capital challenges for the profession, including "stepped-up competition for talent; a rising sense of insecurity; a growing demand for evidence-based, data-driven HR practice and the growing complexity of government legislation and regulations."[1] In a global business world, all employees, including HR staff, must have basic technical knowledge; in addition, they must also possess proficiency in other critical behavioral competencies that allow for the effective application of that knowledge.

Workplace leaders are challenged with not just having people who can do the job today but who are prepared to step up when things change tomorrow. For HR talent strategy, workforce planning, organizational design, and employee development to be successful, HR executives and managers need to understand and use competencies effectively.

The definition of these competencies for HR and their associated Proficiency Indicators can be found in the SHRM Body of Competency and Knowledge (or BoCK), which is based on the SHRM Competency Model. The SHRM Competency Model serves as the foundational model for what it takes to be successful in the HR profession, while the BoCK was developed from the model as a blueprint for SHRM certification and educational products and services. Additionally, the SHRM certification process can identify those individuals who are able to apply the necessary knowledge, skills, abilities, and other characteristics (KSAOs) to the workplace.

The use of competencies in managing has increased in the business world as more and more organizations are basing succession plans on competency development, driven by impending turnover of a large number of experienced professionals. This acknowledgement, however, does not come with easy-to-apply guidance for leaders on how to identify, define, and apply competency models and competencies to ensure their current and future HR staffs possess, develop, and use those competencies to drive individual, HR, and business performance.

How to Use This Book

This book is intended to be a user-friendly tool for anyone who is responsible for managing HR employees. Chapters 1 and 2 discuss the value of competencies in business and the SHRM model, including behavioral indicators. Chapter 3 looks at the links between various competencies and HR functions.

If you are already familiar with these concepts and topics and have identified the competencies critical to your employees, department, and businesses success, you might want to jump to Chapter 4, which overviews ways in which you can assess the level of competency your people have.

If you know what you need but are not sure how to develop your HR employees, see Chapters 5 through 8, which include a variety of suggestions for developmental activities you can use or modify to fit your needs.

Say you are not sure about your own competencies as a people developer, read Chapter 9. The chapter focuses on activities you can use to develop your own competencies related to developing other employees.

There is some impact on career levels when considering developmental activities, and development is a key component of succession planning and preparing others for leadership. Chapter 10 explores these aspects.

Appendix A gives a step-by-step approach with chapter references you can draw on at any time to go to the section of the book you need, thus saving you precious time. It also includes Worksheets #1, #2, and #3 you can use to record and organize your data.

Appendix B includes advice from seasoned and certified HR professionals on their experiences in developing their HR reports.

Appendix C is a quick view of the HR Functions list, and Appendix D includes additional information from the SHRM 2017 BoCK related to Proficiency Indicators for different levels of HR staff.

Appendix E includes the SHRM Competency Development Plan.

Throughout the book you will find charts and lists that should make your task of developing your HR people a little easier.

Disclaimer

Much of the material for this book is something of a reorganization of information from the SHRM Competency Model and related SHRM resources as well as the author's own experience as an HR professional for 25-plus years and as a college professor and instructor for the SHRM Learning System. Many of the development suggestions listed here come from personal experience in helping HR professionals develop themselves and from research conducted for two previous books. Some ideas come from other sources and from HR senior colleagues as well as lists of highly rated books and websites The suggestions are just that—suggestions and beginnings that will hopefully trigger more ideas for you in developing HR competencies.

PART I:

The Business Case for Competencies

CHAPTER 1

Challenges Facing HR Departments

It's a generally recognized fact that having the right people leads to business success. In the past, the right people often meant people who had physical skills. Later, it meant people who had a specific education. Today, things are different, HR and business management have become more complex.

Change Happens

Technology developments, global competition, a diverse employee population, ever-changing government regulations, and social and cultural pressures make the role of HR a constant challenge. This chapter will briefly explore changes and the need for workplace competencies. That the world is constantly changing is a little disputed fact. The pace of change affecting business continues to increase. We operate in what some call a VUCA world, a term introduced in the 1990s that means a world that is volatile, uncertain, complex, and ambiguous.[1] This means that employers face a constant struggle to stay viable if they are to have successful organizations. In the past employees were often hired because they had a craft. They had honed specific physical skills to a level that meant they could provide a service to their employer. With the evolution of industrialization and mechanization, top jobs were driven by simply having knowledge. Just possessing a college degree meant that an individual would likely be able to contribute to the workplace and have a job for life.

Today, just having a skill or knowledge is not enough. Most work is no longer physical, and many formerly skilled jobs are done by machines. Information (knowledge/facts) is readily available, almost instantly, due to advances in technology. It takes more for organizations to succeed now, and this will likely be true into the future. Organizations must be able to respond to changes quickly, and having a "great" staff today that has the skills or knowledge to do the work is only good for today.

In the area of technology alone, we face an evolution in the definitions of work and employment driven by interconnected networks and digital disruption. Groups and teams can and do work virtually across the globe using audio and web conferencing services that are easy to use and affordable. Does that mean that work is no longer limited by location or even the physical ability to come to a workplace?

Customers increasingly demand products and services that are delivered quickly and exactly as they want. This trend is driven by online retailers like Amazon. How does this trend change marketing if you own a retail operation? Do you need sales professionals anymore? Can you take advantage of cost reductions often realized by mass production of goods if everyone wants a custom product?

In social networking sites like Pinterest and Facebook, the customers produce the content. Are they still customers, or are they now employees? If they are employees, are they entitled to various protections or benefits?

Self-service HR software allows employees to make changes and choices on benefits on their own; does that mean we don't need HR staff with benefits knowledge?

This interconnectedness, combined with global dependence of business, means that all workplaces are global and includes issues related to different languages and cultures. Conflict and misunderstanding grow along with the positive aspects of diversity. Employers cannot expect to have one approach or one language anymore. An HR staff that has knowledge of U.S. laws and regulations may be at risk when dealing with a facility located in Africa or Germany where laws and expectations may be very different.

Governments, in an effort to manage or control the safety or interests of individuals in today's chaotic business environment, continue to make laws and regulations that often conflict with the reality of business.

One example is the increasing use of freelance or independent contractors in the gig economy. To be effective, organizations need the contributions of many different people. Sometimes those contributions are needed for a short time, so consultants and contractors are used. Since these contributors don't fit the government definition of "employee," they may be seen as victims of abuse because they don't qualify for things like benefits.

Pay is another issue. Establishing regulations like minimum wages might seem like a good thing. But since laws and regulations are created for the "masses" with the ability to standardize, they are one-size-fits-all and don't allow for the flexibility organizations need to succeed.

Employees as consumers are increasingly expecting customized workplaces. They can get what they want outside the workplace, so why not inside? Demands for different pays structures, benefits, training, and even career paths are becoming more common.

For example, HR managers are increasingly reporting the need to design specific benefits for specific individuals. A young, relatively healthy individual may not be impressed with a high-level medical plan as much as she is by the opportunity to attain additional education. Some employees in the child care or elder care age groups want and need flexible schedules more than pay increases.

How Can Business and HR Respond?

Clearly, organizations can no longer just hire and keep employees based on a specific skill or knowledge set. Having skills and knowledge alone is not enough. But does that mean you can't hire at all, that you just "rent" employees from others or contract them as needed? Though this may be a solution, it is not the answer. This approach ignores the values of consistency and corporate memory and the importance of commitment and loyalty.

The answer is to recruit and hire individuals who possess competencies that can be applied to evolving situations and to develop competencies in current employees. Competencies are a combination of skills and knowledge matched with abilities and attributes that allow application to situations. Competencies go beyond the limits of knowledge. Identifying competencies and looking for them in employees allow organizations to better respond to changing environments because they aren't limited to an individual activity or situation.

An example might be the Society for Human Resource Management (SHRM) competency of Business Acumen, which encompasses the KSAOs needed to understand the organization's operations, functions, and external environment and to apply business tools and analyses that inform HR initiatives and operations consistent with the overall strategic direction of the organization.[2] This means that individuals who have this competency don't just know the strategic planning process or how to read a financial statement. Rather, they understand what information is important and how to make changes, and they use systems thinking. This makes them able to respond to changing conditions.

An HR professional who doesn't possess this competency might find it difficult to deal with the evolving definitions of work and employment.

Another advantage of HR professionals developing competencies along with technical skills and knowledge is that it allows the individuals to function in areas outside HR. This increases their potential for advancement and career growth and helps them work collaboratively with other parts of the organization. Going back to Business Acumen: It would be desired in marketing, operations, and other areas and is a critical competency for organizational leaders.

CHAPTER 2.

Essential HR Competencies

How do competencies assist with talent strategy, workforce planning, and organizational design and the rest of HR's role?

By evaluating the goals of the organization and the resulting business plans, organizations can identify competencies necessary to achieve desired results. When competencies are identified, organizations can then work to hire individuals who possess those competencies or develop them in incumbent workers.

Since competencies go beyond knowledge and skills by describing needed behaviors, the fit or the development is likely to be a stronger connection. Organizations can define how they expect work to be done and connect that with setting performance standards and expectations. The use of competencies within an organization makes the work of HR better and, if universally and well applied, helps ensure that the right people do the right things. Competencies truly tie the business to the people and to good HR functions.

With this approach in mind, what are critical or desired competencies necessary for HR professionals? Though many organizations use a competency model to identify core competencies for the total organization, each job and department will have specific competencies that relate directly to the work each does.

Many agree that the idea of competencies started with David McClelland, who in 1973 argued that competence rather than intelligence is a better predictor of job success.[1] In the mid- to late-1990s, David Ulrich and others began to develop HR competency models that were likely driven by the desire of HR to get a seat at the (leadership) table.[2]

In 2012, the Society for Human Resource Management (SHRM) released a competency model after more than 20 years of research. SHRM used academic resources, global HR professionals, and its own large membership base to validate the content and criteria of the model. The nine HR competencies identified by SHRM will be used as the basis for development suggestions in this book. In 2017, SHRM updated the model to better assist HR professionals.[3]

In the introduction to SHRM's model is a description for behavioral competencies used in this book: A competency is a set of highly interrelated KSAOs that give rise to the behaviors needed to perform a given job effectively.[4] For example, Critical Evaluation, one of the behavioral competencies in the SHRM Competency Model, describes a set of KSAOs including research design knowledge, critical thinking skills, and deductive reasoning abilities. These highly interrelated KSAOs enable HR professionals to collect, compile, analyze, and interpret job-relevant data and information for the purpose of supporting the HR function in their organizations.

A set of competencies that collectively defines the requirements for effective performance in a specific job, profession, or organization may be called a competency model.

FIGURE 2.1: SHRM COMPETENCY MODEL

Competencies can be either technical or behavioral. Technical competencies reflect the knowledge specific to a given profession that is required for a professional in that field to perform a particular role. The HR Expertise competency in the SHRM Competency Model describes the technical knowledge specific to the HR field (such as that associated with talent management, recruiting, or compensation and benefits).

Behavioral competencies, on the other hand, describe the KSAOs that facilitate the application of technical knowledge to job-related behaviors. They are more general in their applicability than the profession-specific technical knowledge that composes HR Expertise. For example, the behavioral competency Communication describes the KSAOs needed to effectively communicate across a range of mediums (for example, e-mail and oral presentations) and with a variety of audiences (for example, internal and external stakeholders).

In sum, technical competencies reflect what knowledge HR professionals apply to their jobs, and behavioral competencies reflect how they apply this knowledge.[5]

Any competency model describes the basic competencies expected for individuals to be successful in the workplace. That said, each job and organization may require varying levels of strength in a particular competency.

For example, Communication as a competency is critical for even the earliest level HR professional. The newer HR professional must be able to clearly communicate organization policies to employees. The executive level HR professional must not only be able to communicate the policy but must also be able to work with other executives to create those policies so that they communicate and support the organization strategies.[6]

As you evaluate your needs, you might want to refer to Appendix D for more detail from the SHRM Body of Competency and Knowledge (BoCK) about Proficiency Indicators for different levels of HR staff.

In a complex, multinational organization, communication at a higher level may be more critical for all HR professionals as opposed to those working in a very small, traditional, stable company in which relationships are more consistent, and people talk every day.

The SHRM Model Includes Nine Competencies

The charts below include a brief definition of each HR competency and the basic behaviors that an individual may display if he or she possesses that competency based on SHRM's model. The Proficiency Indicators (defined as "specific behavioral statements that illustrate effective HR practice") add to the definitions and help you see what successful performance looks like when applying the behavioral competencies. Later chapters will discuss methods for evaluating HR professionals' levels in these areas as well as ideas for helping them further develop their own competencies.

TABLE 2.1: SHRM COMPETENCY MODEL PROFICIENCY INDICATORS

COMPETENCY: COMMUNICATION

Definition	The knowledge, skills, abilities and other characteristics (KSAOs) needed to effectively craft and deliver concise and informative communications, to listen to and address the concerns of others, and to transfer and translate information from one level or unit of the organization to another.
Proficiency Indicators	• Presents needed information to stakeholders and refrains from presenting unneeded information.
	• Uses an understanding of the audience to craft the content of communications (e.g., translates technical jargon), and chooses the best medium of communication.
	• Uses appropriate business terms and vocabulary.
	• Ensures that the delivered message is clear and understood by the listener.
	• Crafts clear, organized, effective, error-free messages.
	• Creates persuasive and compelling arguments.
	• Effectively communicates HR programs, practices, and policies to both HR and non-HR employees.
	• Helps non-HR managers communicate HR issues.
	• Voices support for HR and organizational initiatives in communications with stakeholders.
	• Effectively communicates with senior HR leaders.
	• Listens actively and empathetically to others' views and concerns.
	• Welcomes the opportunity to hear competing points of view and does not take criticism personally.
	• Seeks further information to clarify ambiguity.
	• Promptly responds to and addresses stakeholder communications.
	• Interprets and understands the context of, motives for, and reasoning in received communications.
	• Solicits feedback from senior leaders in other business units about the HR function.

CONTINUED ON NEXT PAGE

TABLE 2.1: SHRM COMPETENCY MODEL PROFICIENCY INDICATORS CONTINUED

COMPETENCY: GLOBAL AND CULTURAL EFFECTIVENESS

Definition	The knowledge, skills, abilities and other characteristics (KSAOs) needed to value and consider the perspectives and backgrounds of all parties, to interact with others in a global context, and to promote a diverse and inclusive workplace.
Proficiency Indicators	• Demonstrates a general awareness and understanding of and respect for cultural differences and issues. • Adapts behavior to navigate different cultural conditions, situations, and people. • Demonstrates acceptance of colleagues from different cultures. • Promotes the benefits of a diverse and inclusive workforce. • Promotes inclusion in daily interactions with others. • Conducts business with an understanding of and respect for cross-cultural differences in customs and acceptable behaviors. • Demonstrates an understanding, from a global perspective, of the organization's line of business. • Tailors HR initiatives to local needs by applying an understanding of cultural differences. • Conducts business with an understanding of and respect for differences in rules, laws, regulations, and accepted business operations and practices. • Applies knowledge of global trends when implementing or maintaining HR programs, practices, and policies. • Operates with a global mindset while remaining sensitive to local issues and needs. • Manages contradictory or paradoxical practices, policies, and cultural norms, to ensure harmony and success across a dispersed workforce. • Supports an organizational culture that values diversity and promotes inclusion. • Uses the organization's policies and philosophy toward diversity and inclusion to inform business decisions and implementation of HR programs, practices, and policies. • Designs, recommends, implements, and/or audits HR programs, practices, and policies intended to ensure diversity and inclusion. • Ensures that HR programs, practices, and policies are applied consistently and respectfully to all staff.

COMPETENCY: RELATIONSHIP MANAGEMENT

Definition	The knowledge, skills, and abilities and other characteristics (KSAOs) needed to create and maintain a network of professional contacts within and outside of the organization, to build and maintain relationships, to work as an effective member of a team, and to manage conflict while supporting the organization.
Proficiency Indicators	• Develops and maintains a network of professional contacts within the organization, including peers in both HR and non-HR roles, HR customers, and stakeholders. • Develops and maintains a network of external partners (e.g., vendors). • Develops and maintains a network of professional colleagues in the HR community at large, for professional development and to fill business needs (e.g., identification of new talent). • Develops and maintains mutual trust and respect with colleagues. • Develops and maintains a pattern of reciprocal exchanges of support, information, and other valued resources with colleagues. • Demonstrates concern for the well-being of colleagues. • Establishes a strong and positive reputation, within and outside the organization, as an open and approachable HR professional. • Ensures that all stakeholder voices are heard and acknowledged. • Identifies and leverages areas of common interest among stakeholders, to foster the success of HR initiatives. • Develops working relationships with supervisors and HR leaders by promptly and effectively responding to work assignments, communicating goal progress and project needs, and managing work activities. • Builds engaged relationships with team members through trust, task-related support, and direct communication. • Fosters collaboration and open communication among stakeholders and team members. • Supports a team-oriented organizational culture. • Creates and/or participates in project teams comprised of HR and non-HR employees. • Embraces opportunities to lead a team. • Identifies and fills missing or unfulfilled team roles. • Resolves and/or mediates conflicts in a respectful, appropriate, and impartial manner, and refers them to a higher level when warranted. • Identifies and addresses the underlying causes of conflict. • Facilitates difficult interactions among employees to achieve optimal outcomes. • Encourages productive and respectful task-related conflict, using it to facilitate change.

CONTINUED ON NEXT PAGE

TABLE 2.1: SHRM COMPETENCY MODEL PROFICIENCY INDICATORS CONTINUED

Proficiency Indicators continued	• Serves as a positive role model for productive conflict. • Identifies and resolves conflict that is counterproductive or harmful. • Maintains a professional demeanor during negotiation discussions. • Applies an understanding of the needs, interests, issues, and bargaining position of all parties to negotiation discussions. • Offers appropriate concessions to promote progress toward an agreement. • Adheres to applicable negotiation- and bargaining-related laws and regulations. • Evaluates progress toward an agreement. • Identifies an ideal solution or end state for negotiations, monitors progress toward that end state, and ends negotiations when appropriate.

COMPETENCY: BUSINESS ACUMEN

Definition	The knowledge, skills, abilities, and other characteristics (KSAOs) needed to understand the organization's operations, functions, and external environment, and to apply business tools and analyses that inform HR initiatives and operations consistent with the overall strategic direction of the organization.
Proficiency Indicators	• Uses organizational and external resources to learn about the organization's business operations, functions, products, and services. • Uses organizational and external resources to learn about the political, economic, social, technological, legal, and environmental (PESTLE) trends that influence the organization. • Applies knowledge of the organization's business operations, functions, products, and services, in order to implement HR solutions and inform business decisions. • Applies knowledge of the organization's industry and the political, economic, social, technological, legal, and environmental (PESTLE) trends, in order to implement HR solutions and inform HR decisions. • Uses cost-benefit analysis, organizational metrics, and key performance indicators to inform business decisions. • Applies principles of finance, marketing, economics, sales, technology, law, and business systems to internal HR programs, practices, and policies. • Uses human resource information systems (HRIS) and business technology to solve problems and address needs. • Demonstrates an understanding of the relationship between effective HR and effective core business functions. • Aligns decisions with HR's and the organization's strategic direction and goals. • Makes the business case, or provides the data to build the case, for HR initiatives and their influence on efficient and effective organizational functioning (e.g., ROI for HR initiatives).

COMPETENCY: CONSULTATION

Definition	The knowledge, skills, abilities and other characteristics (KSAOs) needed to work with organizational stakeholders in evaluating business challenges and identifying opportunities for the design, implementation, and evaluation of change initiatives, and to build ongoing support for HR solutions that meet the changing needs of customers and the business.
Proficiency Indicators	• Develops an understanding of the organization's current and future HR challenges, and helps to identify HR needs and opportunities for improvement. • Identifies current and future HR-related threats and liabilities. • Identifies existing HR programs, practices, and policies that impede or support business success. • Offers, in partnership with stakeholders, HR solutions for business needs that are creative, innovative, effective, and based on best practices and/or research. • Provides guidance to non-HR managers regarding HR practices, compliance, laws, regulations, and ethics. • Defines clear goals and outcomes for HR solutions, using them to drive solution design. • Provides guidance to non-HR managers and business unit teams on implementation of HR-related solutions. • Works with business partners to overcome obstacles to implementation of HR solutions. • Provides follow-up to and ongoing support for implementation of HR solutions, to ensure their continued effectiveness. • Ensures that implementation of HR solutions adheres to defined goals and outcomes. • Recommends ways to improve HR programs, practices, and policies. • Promotes buy-in among organizational stakeholders when implementing change initiatives. • Builds buy-in among staff for organizational change. • Aligns and deploys HR programs to support change initiatives. • Identifies, defines, and clarifies customer needs and requirements, and reports on the status of HR services provided and results achieved. • Responds promptly, courteously, and openly to customer requests, and takes ownership of customer needs. • Identifies and resolves risks and early-stage problems in meeting customer needs. • Manages interactions with vendors and suppliers to maintain service quality.

CONTINUED ON NEXT PAGE

TABLE 2.1: SHRM COMPETENCY MODEL PROFICIENCY INDICATORS CONTINUED

COMPETENCY: CRITICAL EVALUATION

Definition	The knowledge, skills, abilities and other characteristics (KSAOs) needed to collect and analyze qualitative and quantitative data, and to interpret and promote findings that evaluate HR initiatives and inform business decisions and recommendations.
Proficiency Indicators	• Demonstrates an understanding of the importance of using data to inform business decisions and recommendations. • Promotes the importance of evidence-based decision-making. • Promotes the importance of validating HR programs, practices, and policies to ensure that they achieve desired outcomes. • Identifies decision points that can be informed by data and evidence. • Maintains working knowledge of data collection, research methods, benchmarks, and HR metrics. • Identifies sources of the most relevant data for solving organizational problems and answering questions. • Gathers data using appropriate methods (e.g., surveys, focus groups) to inform and monitor organizational solutions. • Scans external sources for data relevant to the organization (e.g., risks, economic and environmental factors). • Benchmarks HR initiatives and outcomes against the organization's competition and other relevant comparison groups. • Maintains working knowledge of statistics and measurement concepts. • Identifies potentially misleading or flawed data. • Conducts analyses to identify evidence-based best practices, evaluate HR initiatives, and determine critical findings. • Maintains objectivity when interpreting data. • Reports key findings to senior business and HR leaders. • Uses research findings to evaluate different courses of action and their impact on the organization. • Applies data-driven knowledge and best practices from one situation to the next, as appropriate. • Ensures that HR programs, practices, and policies reflect research findings and best practices. • Objectively examines HR programs, practices, and policies in light of data.

COMPETENCY: ETHICAL PRACTICE

Definition	The knowledge, skills, and abilities and other characteristics (KSAOs) needed to navigate the organization and accomplish HR goals, to create a compelling vision and mission for HR that aligns with the strategic direction and culture of the organization, to lead and promote organizational change, to manage the implementation and execution of HR initiatives, and to promote the role of HR as a key business partner.
Proficiency Indicators	• Shows consistency between espoused and enacted values. • Acknowledges mistakes and demonstrates accountability for actions. • Recognizes personal biases and the biases of others, and takes steps to increase self-awareness. • Serves as a role model of personal integrity and high ethical standards. • Does not take adverse actions based on personal biases. • Maintains privacy, in compliance with laws and regulations mandating a duty to report unethical behavior. • Uses discretion appropriately when communicating sensitive information, and informs stakeholders of the limits of confidentiality and privacy. • Maintains current knowledge of ethics laws, standards, legislation, and emerging trends that may affect organizational HR practice. • Leads HR investigations of employees in a thorough, timely, and impartial manner. • Establishes oneself as credible and trustworthy. • Applies, and challenges when necessary, the organization's ethics and integrity policies. • Manages political and social pressures when making decisions and when implementing and enforcing HR programs, practices, and policies. • Provides open, honest, and constructive feedback to colleagues when situations involving questions of ethics arise. • Empowers all employees to report unethical behaviors and conflicts of interest without fear of reprisal. • Takes steps to mitigate the influence of bias in HR and business decisions. • Maintains appropriate levels of transparency for HR programs, practices, and policies. • Identifies, evaluates, and communicates to leadership potential ethical risks and conflicts of interest. • Ensures that staff members have access to and understand the organization's ethical standards and policies.

CONTINUED ON NEXT PAGE

TABLE 2.1: SHRM COMPETENCY MODEL PROFICIENCY INDICATORS CONTINUED

COMPETENCY: LEADERSHIP AND NAVIGATION

Definition	The knowledge, skills, and abilities and other characteristics (KSAOs) needed to navigate the organization and accomplish HR goals, to create a compelling vision and mission for HR that aligns with the strategic direction and culture of the organization, to lead and promote organizational change, to manage the implementation and execution of HR initiatives, and to promote the role of HR as a key business partner.
Proficiency Indicators	• Demonstrates an understanding of formal and informal work roles, leader goals and interests, and relationships among employees. • Facilitates communication and decision-making necessary to implement initiatives. • Uses an understanding of the organization's processes, systems, and policies to facilitate the successful implementation of HR initiatives. • Uses awareness and understanding of the organization's political environment and culture to implement HR initiatives. • Embraces and supports the business unit's and/or organization's culture, values, mission, and goals. • Defines actionable goals for the development and implementation of HR programs, practices, and policies that support the strategic vision of HR and the organization. • Identifies opportunities to improve HR operations that better align with and support the strategic vision of HR and the organization. • Supports the implementation of HR programs, practices, and policies that uphold the strategic vision of HR and the organization. • Defines and elaborates project requirements set forth by senior leadership. • Sets and monitors project goals and progress milestones. • Manages project budgets and resources. • Identifies and develops solutions for overcoming obstacles to the successful completion of projects. • Identifies and monitors the resources necessary to implement and maintain HR projects. • Identifies when resource allocation is inconsistent with project needs and make adjustments as necessary. • Demonstrates agility and adaptability when project requirements, goals, or constraints change. • Builds credibility as an HR expert within and outside of the organization. • Promotes buy-in among organizational stakeholders for HR initiatives. • Motivates HR staff and other stakeholders to support HR's vision and goals. • Serves as an advocate for the organization or employees, when appropriate, to ensure advancement of the organization's strategic direction and goals.

COMPETENCY: HR EXPERTISE (HR KNOWLEDGE)– INCLUDES HR FUNCTIONAL AREAS. SEE APPENDIX C FOR DETAILS ON THE FUNCTIONAL AREAS.

Definition	The knowledge of principles, practices and functions of effective human resource management.
Proficiency Indicators	• Remains current on relevant laws, legal rulings and regulations. • Maintains up-to-date knowledge of general HR practices, strategy and technology. • Demonstrates a working knowledge of critical human resource functions. • Prioritizes work duties for maximum efficiency. • Develops and utilizes best practices. • Delivers customized human resource solutions for organizational challenges. • Seeks professional HR development. • Seeks process improvement through numerous resources. • Utilizes core business and HR-specific technologies to solve business challenges.

The SHRM Competency Model groups the Behavioral Competencies into Clusters. Since the clusters are made up of related competencies, the developmental activities for each may overlap. Individual employees may have strengths or weakness in a particular cluster, so it is appropriate to explore them together for the purposes of this book.

The Groupings are:

- **Interpersonal.** Includes Communication, Global and Cultural Effectiveness, and Relationship Management.
- **Business.** Includes Business Acumen, Consultation, and Critical Evaluation.
- **Leadership.** Includes Ethical Practice and Leadership and Navigation.

This book will focus on the eight Behavioral Competencies since they are typically the areas where managers need the most help. HR Expertise, SHRM's ninth area includes technical HR which managers are more comfortable in developing in their reports. In addition there is a lot of material and guidance in that competency development

Here is a list of the SHRM competencies along with behaviors that are considered Proficiency Indicators for HR professionals in general. For information on indicators for higher-level HR professionals, refer to Appendix D.

So What Do You and Your Employees Need?

Based on feedback from HR management colleagues, it is best to use multiple sources for deciding which HR competencies you need for your particular situation, person, or group of employees.

Starting with well-researched and consistently updated sources like the SHRM Competency Model, you should then evaluate your organization's needs. As mentioned earlier, you need to understand your organization and its goals, plans, and strategies. Then you can determine the key competencies your people need.

Your organization may have identified core organizational competencies, and if you work in a large organization in which you report to a department head, he or she may have determined key competencies for the department. As you determine your staff needs, you can look to align them with these organizational competencies.

Worksheet #1 in Appendix A can be used to record information on the competencies that you have identified for your employee team. It includes a list of the SHRM HR competencies as well as a place to document your company's or department's key competencies. In addition, the worksheet contains cells where you can document the strengths and development needs you have for your team. Keep in mind that all of the HR competencies are likely desired in a good HR function, but by prioritizing them as desired, priority, or core, you can focus on the most important to develop right now.

Chapter 4 will present information on how to assess the competencies of HR professionals. You can use Worksheet #2 in the Appendix to record assessment results for each employee and to document a development plan. Also, Appendix D includes the SHRM Competency Development form if you are strictly following the SHRM model.

In Chapter 9 the discussion shifts to what competencies are critical for you as the individual responsible for developing others. Though a number of competencies are necessary for you to develop to help your staff develop theirs, these four, based on the author's experience and research and discussion with other HR professionals, are the most important of the HR behavioral competencies:

TABLE 2.2: CRITICAL COMPETENCIES

Business Acumen	The knowledge, skills, abilities and other characteristics (KSAOs) needed to understand the organization's operations, functions, and external environment, and to apply business tools and analyses that inform HR initiatives and operations consistent with the overall strategic direction of the organization.
Consultation	The knowledge, skills, abilities and other characteristics (KSAOs) needed to work with organizational stakeholders in evaluating business challenges and identifying opportunities for the design, implementation, and evaluation of change initiatives, and to build ongoing support for HR solutions that meet the changing needs of customers and the business.
Critical Evaluation	The knowledge, skills, abilities and other characteristics (KSAOs) needed to collect and analyze qualitative and quantitative data, and to interpret and promote findings that evaluate HR initiatives and inform business decisions and recommendations.
Relationship Management	The knowledge, skills, abilities and other characteristics (KSAOs) needed to create and maintain a network of professional contacts within and outside of the organization, to build and maintain relationships, to work as an effective member of a team, and to manage conflict while supporting the organization.

In addition to these behavioral competencies, the HR Expertise functional area of Learning and Development is essential for managing development.

As we explore the activities you can use for your employees, think about these four competencies and how you might enhance or develop them yourself. Chapter 9 will go into more detail on how you can develop the necessary competencies helpful for developing others. You may uncover other competencies that are advantageous for your own development.

Worksheet #3 in the Appendix is a form you can use to develop a plan for your employee or for yourself.

PART II:

Linking HR Competencies to Business Outcomes

CHAPTER 3.

Aligning HR Functions with Competencies

Business professionals and HR managers often struggle with the connection between HR functions and HR competencies. There are obvious links, but on looking at the descriptions of the SHRM HR competencies in Chapter 2, managers might think that all competencies relate to all functions. Though this is true to a point, specific competencies connect more directly to functional areas. HR Expertise (the HR Technical Competency) describes functions, so we will explore the links between only the other eight behavioral competencies and the functional areas.

This chapter is meant to help you develop a better understanding of the competencies. It can also help you build a communication strategy for securing resources and support from your management so that you can carry out your employee development plans. In addition, it can help you determine which HR competencies are most important to your group depending on which functions you have in your group.

For the purposes of this book, we will use information from the 2017 SHRM Body of Competency and Knowledge (BoCK). An additional source is the SHRM Learning System for information on the relationship between behavioral competencies and HR functions described in the technical competency.[1]

The SHRM BoCK lists under HR Expertise (the technical competencies) 15 HR functional areas divided into three groups: People, Organization, and Workplace. Chapter 2 mentioned these functional areas, and Appendix C includes a concise listing. In this chapter we will look at the definition of each functional area and a proficiency indicator for each associated behavioral competency. Keep in mind, these are only suggestions. Other competencies may apply or be more important for your particular group or organization.

For example, Talent Acquisition and Retention, Business Acumen, Critical Evaluation, and Consultation are called out as important for effective work. But what if you have a very diverse, global business? In that case, Global and Cultural Effectiveness may be as, or more relevant, than the other three mentioned. As you develop your plans as outlined in Chapter 2, you may want to go beyond the suggestions to better fit your employee's specific needs.

People Group

Functional Area #1 HR Strategic Planning involves the activities necessary for developing, implementing, and managing the strategic direction required to achieve organizational success and to create value for stakeholders.

   Related behavioral competency proficiency indicator:
- **Business Acumen.** Aligns decisions with HR's and the organization's strategic direction and goals.
- **Critical Evaluation.** Ensures that HR programs, practices and policies reflect research findings and best practices
- **Consultation.** Identifies existing HR programs, practices and policies that impede or support business success.

Functional Area #2 Talent Acquisition encompasses the activities involved in building and maintaining a workforce that meets the needs of the organization.

   Related behavioral competency proficiency indicator:
- **Business Acumen.** Applies knowledge of the organization's business operations, functions, products and services, in order to implement HR solutions and inform business decisions (such as talent acquisition decisions).
- **Critical Evaluation.** Benchmarks HR initiatives and outcomes (such as those in talent acquisition) against the organization's competition and other relevant comparison groups.
- **Consultation.** Provides guidance to non-HR managers regarding HR practices (such as talent acquisition), compliance, laws, regulations and ethics.

Functional Area #3 Employee Engagement & Retention refers to activities aimed at retaining high-performing talent, solidifying and improving the relationship between employees and the organization, creating a thriving and energized workforce, and developing effective strategies to address appropriate performance expectations from employees at all levels.

   Related behavioral competency proficiency indicator:
- **Communication.** Effectively communicates HR programs, practices and policies to both HR and non-HR employees.
- **Relationship Management.** Fosters collaboration and open communication among stakeholders and team members.
- **Consultation.** Works with business partners to overcome obstacles to implementation of HR solutions (such as engagement and retention efforts).

Functional Area #4 Learning & Development activities to enhance the KSAOs and competencies of the workforce in order to meet the organization's business needs.

   Related behavioral competency proficiency indicator:
- **Business Acumen.** Applies principles of finance, marketing, economics, sales, technology, law and business systems to internal HR programs (such as learning & development), practices and policies.
- **Critical Evaluation.** Conducts analyses to identify evidence-based best practices,

evaluate HR initiatives and determine critical findings.
- **Relationship Management.** Identifies and leverages areas of common interest among stakeholders, to foster the success of HR initiatives.

Functional Area #5 Total Rewards encompasses the design and implementation of compensation systems and benefit packages, which employers use to attract and retain employees.

    Related behavioral competency proficiency indicator:
- **Business Acumen.** Makes the business case, or provides the data to build the case, for HR initiatives and their influence on efficient and effective organizational functioning (e.g., ROI for HR initiatives).
- **Critical Evaluation.** Demonstrates an understanding of the importance of using data to inform business decisions and recommendations (such as those regarding the total reward system).
- **Communication.** Effectively communicates HR programs, practices and policies to both HR and non-HR employees.

Organization Group

Functional Area #6 Structure of the HR Function encompasses the people, processes, theories, and activities involved in the delivery of HR-related services that create and drive organizational effectiveness.

    Related behavioral competency proficiency indicator:
- **Business Acumen.** Applies knowledge of the organization's business operations, functions, products and services, in order to implement HR solutions and inform business decisions.
- **Critical Evaluation.** Ensures that HR programs, practices and policies reflect research findings and best practices.
- **Consultation.** Aligns and deploys HR programs to support change initiatives.

Functional Area #7 Organizational Effectiveness & Development concerns the overall structure and functionality of the organization, and involves measurement of long- and short-term effectiveness and growth of people and processes and implementation of necessary organizational change initiatives.

    Related behavioral competency proficiency indicator:
- **Business Acumen.** Demonstrates an understanding of the relationship between effective HR and effective core business functions.
- **Critical Evaluation.** Uses research findings to evaluate different courses of action and their impacts on the organization.
- **Relationship Management.** Develops and maintains a pattern of reciprocal exchanges of support, information and other valued resources with colleagues.

Functional Area #8 Workforce Management includes HR practices and initiatives that allow the organization to meet its talent needs (for example, workforce planning, succession planning) and to close critical competency gaps.

Related behavioral competency proficiency indicator:

- **Business Acumen.** Applies knowledge of the organization's industry and PESTLE trends, in order to implement HR solutions and inform HR decisions.
- **Critical Evaluation.** Identifies sources of the most relevant data for solving organizational problems and answering questions (such as those used in workforce management).
- **Relationship Management.** Identifies and fills missing or unfulfilled team roles.

Functional Area #9 Employee & Labor Relations refers to any dealings between the organization and its employees regarding the terms and conditions of employment.

Related behavioral competency proficiency indicator:

- **Ethical Practice.** Manages political and social pressures when making decisions and when implementing and enforcing HR programs, practices and policies.
- **Relationship Management.** Applies an understanding of the needs, interests, issues and bargaining position of all parties to negotiation discussions.
- **Critical Evaluation.** Identifies sources of the most relevant data for solving organizational problems and answering questions, such as those related to terms and conditions of employment.

Functional Area #10 Technology Management involves the use of existing, new, and emerging technologies (for example, cloud computing, electronic communications, contingency systems) to support the HR function and the development and implementation of policies and procedures that govern the use of technologies in the workplace.

Related behavioral competency proficiency indicator:

- **Business Acumen.** Uses HR information systems (HRIS) and business technology to solve problems and address needs.
- **Critical Evaluation.** Maintains working knowledge of data collection, research methods, benchmarks and HR metrics, including the appropriate technology for collecting and analyzing HR-related data.
- **Communication.** Uses an understanding of the audience to craft the content of communications (e.g., translates technical jargon), and chooses the best medium (such as the most appropriate technological solution) for communication.

Workplace Group

Functional Area #11 HR in the Global Context focuses on the role of the HR professional in managing global workforces to achieve organizational objectives.

Related behavioral competency proficiency indicator:

- **Communication.** Interprets and understands the context of, motives for and reasoning in received communications (e.g., considering national, geographic or cultural differences).

- **Global and Cultural Effectiveness.** Adapts behavior to navigate different cultural conditions, situations and people.
- **Consultation.** Develops an understanding of the organization's current and future HR challenges (such as those in a global context), and helps to identify HR needs and opportunities for improvement.

Functional Area #12 Diversity & Inclusion encompasses activities that create opportunities for the organization to leverage the unique backgrounds and characteristics of all employees to contribute to its success.

Related behavioral competency proficiency indicator:
- **Ethical Practice.** Takes steps to mitigate the influence of bias in HR and business decisions.
- **Relationship Management.** Identifies and leverages areas of common interest among stakeholders, to foster the success of HR initiatives.
- **Communication.** Listens actively and empathetically to others' views and concerns.

Functional Area #13 Risk Management is the identification, assessment, and prioritization of risks and the application of resources, accordingly, to minimize, monitor, and control the probability and impact of those risks accordingly.

Related behavioral competency proficiency indicator:
- **Business Acumen.** Uses cost-benefit analysis, organizational metrics and key performance indicators to inform business decisions.
- **Critical Evaluation.** Scans external sources for data relevant to the organization (e.g., risks, economic and environmental factors).
- **Communication.** Crafts clear, organized, effective and error-free messages.

Functional Area #14 Corporate Social Responsibility represents the organization's commitment to operate in an ethical and sustainable manner by engaging in activities that promote and support philanthropy, transparency, sustainability, and ethically sound governance practices.

Related behavioral competency proficiency indicator:
- **Consultation.** Provides guidance to non-HR managers regarding HR practices, compliance, laws, regulations and ethics.
- **Relationship Management.** Develops and maintains a network of professional contacts within the organization, including peers in both HR and non-HR roles, HR customers and stakeholders.
- **Global and Cultural Effectiveness.** Operates with a global mindset while remaining sensitive to local issues and needs.

Functional Area #15 U.S. Employment Law & Regulations deals with the knowledge and application of all relevant laws and regulations in the United States relating to employment. These provisions set the parameters and limitations for each HR functional area, and for organizations overall.

Related behavioral competency proficiency indicator:

- **Ethical Practice.** Maintains current knowledge of ethics laws, standards, legislation and emerging trends that may affect organizational HR practice.
- **Critical Evaluation.** Demonstrates an understanding of the importance of using data to inform business decisions and recommendations, such as the interpretation of legal compliance information and data.
- **Leadership and Navigation.** Uses an understanding of the organization's processes, systems and policies to facilitate the successful implementation of HR initiatives.

Next Steps

As noted in Chapter 2, you need to determine priorities when deciding the areas you want to focus on for your employees' development. Even if you have very early level people who are weak in many areas, you can't develop everything at once, and all employees will have strengths and weaknesses. As discussed before, examine the priorities of your organization related to HR competencies and the needs of your group. Using the information in this chapter, you can determine critical needs based on the functions that are most important to a position and the competencies related to those functions. This will help you complete Worksheet #1: HR Competencies Needed for Your HR Function, in Appendix A.

As noted at the beginning of this chapter, this material is intended to provide an understanding of the relationship between HR functions as organized in the HR Expertise (HR Knowledge) technical competency and the SHRM HR behavioral competencies. It is not all inclusive, and as you work through this planning, you may come to different conclusions about competencies you need and the functions that your employees perform. The key is to see that good performance takes more than just knowledge and skills and that the development of competencies provides flexible approaches to our ever-changing business world and future success.

Next we will discuss how to evaluate the level of competency that an individual or a team might currently possess so that you can start your development plans.

CHAPTER 4

Assessing Proficiencies

Now that you think you know which competencies you need, how do you know if your employees (and candidates for hire) have those competencies? If the competencies are present, what levels do your employees possess? What are their strengths and areas for development? In this chapter we will explore a number of methods for evaluating whether an individual possesses a particular competency, again using the SHRM Competency Model as the basis. We will also talk about evaluating candidates for employment as well as determining the levels of current employees.

As mentioned in Chapter 2, we sometimes think that our team or one of our employees is weak (or even strong) in a particular competency, but on taking a closer look we find something else. For example, managers often say, "He just doesn't have good Relationship Management," when in reality the individual may be lacking in Communication or Global and Cultural Effectiveness competencies. In addition, at times an employee may actually have a competency, but, for other reasons, she does not display behaviors that verify it. Maybe she has emotional issues or personal problems or lacks necessary resources to show that she is competent in a particular area.

This closer look through a variety of assessment approaches may reveal the fact that we need to change something else in the work environment rather than develop a competency. Be prepared to do rewrites on Worksheet #3 during the assessment step.

A Word of Caution

Any time you evaluate a candidate or employee, make sure you are being fair, consistent, and legally compliant. Since we all have unconscious biases, they can affect how we judge individuals. For this reason, you should never base any decisions on hiring, promotion, training, or terminating on one assessment alone. You should also make sure the assessment has validity and reliability.

In addition, you need to provide opportunities consistently to all candidates or employees to ensure fairness. We may be tempted sometimes, as we look at competencies, to focus on the star performers and their development, but we need to provide opportunities to everyone. And sometimes the employee who you think is not a star may start to shine with just receiving attention during the assessment process.

Assessing Current Employees

In Chapter 2 we discussed how to identify the strengths and weaknesses you have in your total current employee group matched against the competencies you need. But all employees are not equal in terms of their levels, so how can we diagnose development needs for each person?

One of the first approaches to evaluating competencies is to look at current and past performance.

Direct Methods

Direct methods include meeting with employees, observation, and meeting with co-workers, customers, managers and supervisors. Observing employees doing their work, asking employees questions (you can use the questions provided later in this chapter for candidates), or asking employees to perform a task or assignment meant to demonstrate competencies. Let's look at each of these direct methods.

Meeting with Employees

The most direct method for determining competencies is discussing them with employees. The advantages of this approach include engaging employees in the process and helping them understand what is important, in your judgment, for their future success.

Some organizations have a career or development discussion as a part of their performance management process. If yours does, you can use this as an opportunity to assess competencies as long as employees have a high level of trust in the system and your own relationship management capabilities are strong. You should let employees know that competencies are meaningful to career and job success.

You can use some of the interview questions provided for candidates later in this chapter to generate discussion with employees and to determine their levels. Just as you would with candidates, keep good notes about their responses and their questions.

Observation

As you observe your employees working, note behaviors and identify competencies that are exhibited. Using the Proficiency Indicators in Chapter 2, think about those displayed by the employees and record your thoughts. Be sure to include the level of success the employees accomplish in their work.

For example, you have determined that the competency Relationship Management is critical for a particular function: benefits. One of the Proficiency Indicators for that competency in the chart in Chapter 2 is: "demonstrates approachability and openness."

You noticed during your benefits open enrollment period that employees seemed to gravitate to team member A of your benefits team when asking questions, but they seemed to avoid team member B. Member B may need some work on the Relationship Management competency. To determine the level of help he may need, consider these questions: Does member B lack knowledge, skills, or abilities that would make him better at Relationship Management, or is something else affecting his behaviors? For example, is he a newer employee who is not yet recognized by others as a resource? Knowing more will help you choose the appropriate developmental activities for member B. We will discuss development methods in future chapters.

You can also plan ahead to observe an employee on the job. Before observing any employee, you should determine the behaviors you are looking for and create a score sheet for yourself that lists the behaviors you expect the employee to display. Observe with as little disruption as possible. If you are commonly in the work area, observation without disruption will be easier. If not, you may want to watch the work several times before making a judgment about the level of proficiency that the employee exhibits. You don't want your presence to influence the employee's behaviors.

You can also observe assignments or activities that are not a part of the daily job. Say you want to know your employee's level of competency in Critical Evaluation. One of the Proficiency Indicators under Data Gathering is gathers critical information. You might assign the employee to a team that is investigating a new human resource information system (HRIS) system. You can then look at how well the individual contributes to data gathering on the team.

Make sure you take good notes on the behaviors you see, and try to be objective and specific in recording your observations.

Meeting with Co-workers, Customers, Managers, Supervisors

Much like in meetings with individual employees, you can obtain a lot of information about behaviors that indicate competencies by meeting with others who work with an individual. Plan questions ahead of time, basing them both on the actual behaviors and on the relationship of the employee with his or her co-workers.

Cautions here include which co-workers and customers you approach and how you approach them. You need honest answers based on specific examples if you are going to use the information. It is best to use this method along with others to ensure fairness in case a colleague or customer reveals negative motives toward the employee you are evaluating.

Indirect Indicators

Review of Performance Documents

If you have an effective performance management system in place, you may be able to look at past performance reviews of employees to assess their competencies. This would include looking at past ratings of and comments about your employees and connecting them to the competency model.

Using the competency definitions and Proficiency Indicators listed in Chapter 2 and considering the information on how competencies are related to business functions in Chapter 3, look for descriptions of related performance in the reviews.

For example, one of your employees may have done a particularly good job in developing a new benefits program that supported the goals of recruiting and retaining employees. This performance may indicate that the employee is strong in both Consultation and Business Acumen since acceptance of the program likely hinged on those competencies.

The key here is to make sure your performance management system is valid and reliable before pinning your judgments on it. If it is not well developed or if your managers don't use it effectively, the data produced by the system may not be useful and could lead to bad decisions or discrimination claims.

Search Learning Management Systems

Today organizations may have systems that track training and development. Mining the information in these systems may help identify employees' level of competency. Remember that a competency includes knowledge, skills, and abilities, so past education or training, especially if it included assessments that gauge the level of learning, may give you useful data.

Review Career History

Review of past positions at both your organization and in previous jobs may also reveal information about competencies. The more you know about the past job or organization, the better. Be careful not to assume too much from job titles. You may want to combine this method with questioning your employees or their past supervisors to determine what competencies they developed in what positions.

Certifications

Professional certifications can indicate that an individual has various competencies. It is important to understand the certification and how it was acquired. Some, like the SHRM Certified Professional (SHRM-CP) and SHRM Senior Certified Professional (SHRM-SCP), focus on HR competencies. Other HR generalist certifications, and those for compensation professionals, benefits specialists, or other functions, likely include evaluation of competencies as part of their tests, but it is a good idea to research the certifications your employees have or acquire before assuming what they measure. Chapters 5 through 8 offer information related to certifications for some of the competencies since preparing for a certification can also help an individual develop components of those competencies.

Specific Competency Assessment Tools

In 2014 SHRM released assessment tools for evaluating competencies in HR professionals and HR departments. The tools were developed to complement the SHRM Competency Model, and research from the model lead to the development of questions about each competency. From there, input from subject matter experts (SMEs) further validated the questions in a cognitive lab. The questions were also evaluated for global applicability.

The assessment tools include the Diagnostic-180 Tool, the Diagnostic-360 Tool, and the HR Department Tool. According to SHRM, individuals have used the tools to assess their current level of ability in relation to the SHRM Competency Model. In addition, they can use the tools to decide where to focus their professional development or recertification credits. For example, staff members who find that they have room to improve in Business Acumen from their results can use that data to focus more professional development or recertification credits in that area.

While individuals can benefit from the tools, so too can companies. Corporations have purchased the tools to evaluate the level effectiveness of their HR teams in relation to the SHRM Competency Model. Using either the 180 Tool or 360 Tool for each member of the HR team, an HR leader can produce aggregate reports of the team's strengths and areas of improvement on the eight behavioral competencies. The 180 Tool allows individuals to rate themselves, as well as to directly or indirectly rate their supervisor(s). The 360 Tools allows those same two points of evaluation along with that of peers and direct reports. At the organizational level, results can help HR leaders understand areas of opportunity to better inform training and development plans for their team.

The HR Department Tool is essentially a 360-degree review of the entire HR department for an organization in relation to the SHRM Competency Model. It is commonly referred to as a stakeholder survey since it solicits input on the HR team performance from various levels of the organization. This is the only SHRM Diagnostic that captures input on all nine competencies within the model.

Other assessment tools that call out competencies are available, and working with an assessment center or industrial psychologist may provide additional options. Chapters 5 through 8, which focus on developmental activities, also include suggestions for assessment tools related to each competency.

Assessing Candidates

Though the focus of this book is to help you develop competencies in your current employees, it is valuable to think about how you might assess the desired competencies of candidates as you select them for employment.

Two important thoughts here include a focus on competencies that complement your current group and the use of your analysis going forward to further develop the person you choose. By focusing on the missing competencies, you more quickly bring your group up to the level you want by "hiring in" competencies. The people you hire may even be able to assist in the development of their strongest competencies in your other employees.

When it comes to future development for the new employees, you can focus on what's missing or needs more work in the people you hire. By doing assessments before hiring some of your analysis work is done.

As noted before, use approaches that are valid, reliable, and legally defensible when dealing with employee decisions and particularly so when talking about selection decisions. The use of competency-focused behavioral interview questions is an effective way to evaluate both candidates and current employees. Listed here are suggestions for each competency. The form below can be used to capture answers that you can evaluate after the interview.

Select the questions in Worksheet #4 below that make the most sense for your situation and that focus on your department's and organization's critical or needed competencies. You can make notes related to the interview or the answers you are expecting.

WORKSHEET 4.1: SUGGESTED QUESTIONS FOR EVALUATING CANDIDATE COMPETENCY

QUESTION	ANSWER IDEAS	YOUR NOTES
COMMUNICATION		
At one time or another, we have all had some problems getting our point across when talking with another person (directly or on the telephone). Give me some examples of when this may have happened to you.	Answer should include a focus on listening to the other person, determining what motivates the other person, and then asking clarifying questions. May include waiting for the person to calm down if he or she is upset.	
What different approaches do you use in talking with different people? (How do you know you are getting your point across?)	Listen for an understanding that people differ in understanding based on intellect, original language, life experience, education, etc.	
Tell me about a time you had to coach a manager who was having a problem with an employee. What happened?	Best answer should be a serious situation with positive results. Examples of less success with some "learning" are also good.	
Describe a time when you used your listening skills to "sell" an idea to your boss.	Example is best if it shows an understanding of the boss' perspective and motivations as well as the culture and business needs.	
HR professionals need to keep good documentation. What does this mean?	Listen for a focus on clear and concise written communication as well as detailed information to protect the company from legal risks.	
GLOBAL AND CULTURAL EFFECTIVENESS		
What does "diversity" mean?	Answer should include the realization that diversity is not just race or gender but that everyone is diverse as all individuals are different in some way.	
Tell me about a time that you had to help an employee who was "different" become a part of an organization.	Listen for efforts to educate employees about the value of differences or different thinking.	
Describe a time when others disagreed with you. What did you do?	Look for a willingness to listen and change based on input from others.	
What is the biggest challenge in a diverse working environment? What steps would you take to meet this challenge?	Listen for an understanding of diversity and direct involvement in dealing with diversity problems.	

CONTINUED ON NEXT PAGE

WORKSHEET 4.1: SUGGESTED QUESTIONS FOR EVALUATING CANDIDATE COMPETENCY CONTINUED

QUESTION	ANSWER IDEAS	YOUR NOTES
How did/does your current/former employer approach diversity and inclusion? How have you participated in/supported this approach?	Listen to hear if the past/current environment is like the one at your company. Listen for candidates' feelings about the diversity environment and how they improved the situation.	

RELATIONSHIP MANAGEMENT

QUESTION	ANSWER IDEAS	YOUR NOTES
If I asked the managers and employees at your past positions about you, what would they say?	Answer should include specific information about how they came to the person for help and collaboration. Great answer would include a time when they won a manager or employee over who was skeptical.	
How would you approach becoming a part of our team, if you got this job?	Listen for a plan to meet with and listen to the needs of the managers and an offer of "how can I help?" type questions.	
Describe your professional network and how you maintain it.	Expect to hear about a large network of professionals from human resources and the industry as well as outside both. Good answer would include regular efforts to reach out and grow the network.	
What is HR's role in an organization? Why is it important?	Answer should include reference to how HR should understand the business and contribute to it from the HR perspective. Might include recognition that an HR professional must always maintain a balanced focus on the organization and the employees alike.	
What does customer service mean in HR?	Listen for an understanding that HR needs to serve both management and employees by helping each understand the other to support the organization.	

BUSINESS ACUMEN

QUESTION	ANSWER IDEAS	YOUR NOTES
Give me an example of a time when your knowledge of the business operations was helpful in getting something done.	Answer should include information on how the knowledge was acquired and negotiating abilities.	
How do you use financial, economic or industry information to get support for HR needs?	Look for a true understanding of financial and economic data, not just popular terms.	
How have you made a memorable difference in past business?	Answer is best if the action saved the organization in terms of money or time or helped make money.	

CONTINUED ON NEXT PAGE

WORKSHEET 4.1: SUGGESTED QUESTIONS FOR EVALUATING CANDIDATE COMPETENCY CONTINUED

QUESTION	ANSWER IDEAS	YOUR NOTES
What type of organizational structure (centralized or decentralized) do you prefer and why?	Consider your structure. Centralized would be when decisions are made from the top and there are lots of controls. Decentralized departments are those that are given a lot of latitude to make decisions based on their needs, goals. A company that wants to control costs might be more centralized. A creative customer responsive company less so.	
What do you see as the relationship between "corporate culture" and business success?	Expect a recognition that the culture needs to support the business mission and goals.	

CONSULTATION

Give me an example of a workforce issue you solved.	Listen for the level or difficulty of the problem and the application of HR knowledge.	
Tell me about a time you provided your HR expertise/skills to help solve a company problem.	Look for recognition from other managers and employees that the person is an expert in HR.	
What do you think the phrase "creative problem-solver" means in HR?	Answer should include a perspective that includes inviting ideas from others, not just being "rule" oriented, etc.	

CRITICAL EVALUATION

What was one of the toughest problems you ever solved? What process did you go through to solve it?	Consider the depth of the answer, and look for a step-by-step approach using critical thinking and research.	
How do you analyze different options to determine which is the best alternative?	Answer should include analysis of each alternative, research, working with others.	
Describe for me how your prior positions required you to be proficient in the analysis of technical reports?	Determine if the type of reports is similar to the kind you use.	
How have you approached solving a problem that initially seemed insurmountable?	Look for the business importance of the problem and a logical approach to the resolution as well as collaborating with managers.	
How do you approach researching information to help you make important decisions?	Answer may include professional organizations, experts, managers, employees who do the job, the Internet, professional publications. Look for multiple sources, not just one.	

ETHICAL PRACTICE

Tell me about a time when you have come across a questionable business practice. How did you handle the situation?	Listen for efforts to resolve the problem by investigating confidentially, working with legal counsel, and working with managers.	
Have you ever faced a significant ethical problem at work? How did you handle it?	Look for HR and legal knowledge and aspects like efforts to resolve the problem by investigating confidentially, working with legal counsel, and working with managers.	

CONTINUED ON NEXT PAGE

WORKSHEET 4.1: SUGGESTED QUESTIONS FOR EVALUATING CANDIDATE COMPETENCY CONTINUED

QUESTION	ANSWER IDEAS	YOUR NOTES
Describe a time when you made a mistake at work. How did you deal with this situation, and what was the outcome?	Seriousness of the mistake is important as well as self-acceptance and learning going forward.	
How have you handled situations where someone, employee, vendor, or supplier had a conflict of interest?	Look for understanding of values within the particular industry and including them with the problem resolutions as well as educating others about reducing business risk.	
Explain the phrase "work ethic." How would you describe your work ethic?	Answer should include a dedication to being honest. Listen for a balanced view on dedication to the job and a personal life.	

LEADERSHIP AND NAVIGATION

QUESTION	ANSWER IDEAS	YOUR NOTES
Tell me about a time when you used collaboration to solve a problem.	Expect a workplace problem that included listening, engaging others, and flexibility.	
When should you use consensus decision-making versus voting or directing in HR?	Answer should include an acknowledgement that at times due to business needs or legal restrictions you need to make a directive decision but that consensus is often better because all agree to accept the decision.	
How have you considered you company's culture when participating in a new project or program?	Listen for an example that clearly shows an understanding of the business and the value of selling an idea or moving something forward using that.	
Tell me about a time when you participated in a company-wide project or initiative. What role did you play?	Look for leadership roles and understanding of the business and culture.	
Tell me about a time when you were responsible for an unpopular change, how you approached it and what you learned from it.	Answer should include reference to determining why it was unpopular as well as efforts to engage the people who were dealing with the change in making some decisions.	

HR EXPERTISE

QUESTION	ANSWER IDEAS	YOUR NOTES
How do you stay current on changes in labor laws and regulations?	Listen for recent legal training/education or development program attendance; membership and participation in related HR organizations; references to reading books, websites, HR blogs, etc.	
Tell me what you know about our company/business.	Expect detail based on what might be available via websites or contacts. Reference to similar businesses is good too.	
If you got this position, what would be your biggest challenge as far as learning the business?	Answer should include recognition of areas of lack of experience or knowledge.	
What have you done in the last two years to keep up-to-date with changes in the HR field?	Listen for recent HR training/education or development program attendance; membership and participation in related HR organizations; references to reading books, websites, HR blogs, etc.	

Other Assessment Approaches for Candidates

As with employees, you can use other formal assessments with candidates some of which may be ok to use for selection decisions. SHRM recommends that their tools not be used for selection decisions. Though they are good assessments, they don't likely yet have enough history of use to be considered totally valid and reliable to be defensible in a discrimination complaint situation.

If you want to use pre-employment assessments, you need to verify their validity and reliability, and you should probably not use personality tests to test for competencies because they may not be valid predictors.

References

Similar to the questions you ask co-workers, managers, and customers when evaluating current employees, you can use the same approach when speaking with references for candidates.

Asking professional references questions about past behaviors may give you some sense of the competencies and levels of candidates.

Troubleshooting Problems

What if your employees don't want to develop? What if they can't?

As you go through the process of evaluating your employees, you may come across some individuals who are not motivated to develop themselves. They don't have an interest in moving forward. If you have tried to help them understand the importance of developing themselves, and they're still unwilling, you may have to make some hard decisions.

Can you change their job to use their current competency level? If their reason is a personal challenge, maybe you can wait until they are ready. You don't want to try to resolve their problems, but you may be able to alert them to support systems, employee assistance programs, or other options. Finally, you may need to focus on how you can help them leave, either moving to another part of the organization where their competency levels are a better match or leaving the organization altogether.

But before resorting to helping employees leave the job or organization, be careful because emotional or intellectual limitations may be considered disabilities protected by various laws. Try to develop people to the level they are capable of achieving. Not everyone is able to be the CEO, and your organization only needs one. Different jobs need different levels of competencies.

Record your plans for assessing current employees' competencies in Worksheet #2 in Appendix A—or you can use the form from the SHRM Competency Development Plan in Appendix E).

PART III:

Working through the SHRM Competencies Clusters to Create Development Plans

Once you have determined the critical competencies for individuals in your department and assessed their levels for each, you can set up a plan to help them develop. Worksheet #3: Competency Development Planning Sheet can be used to record that plan. You can also use the form to discuss the developmental activities with each employee, particularly if he or she has not completed the activities by the deadline established by both of you. You should note when you plan to meet next with the employee after developing the plan.

Evaluating Development

It is important to assess the development of employees on a regular basis. You may want to review the assessment methods in Chapter 4 for insights. The selected deadlines listed on employees' development plans may drive this step, but you should be meeting on a regular basis to discuss progress and evaluate next steps.

There are several approaches to initiating the individual development form.

One approach is for you to complete the initial checklist of needed competencies and then have employees identify their strengths and areas for improvement as well as developmental activities. You could then meet and come to a consensus on the activities to pursue, the end date, and the evaluation methods. This approach is likely to engage employees since they will likely feel more responsible for something they have contributed to because it gives them a stake in the development activities.

Another method is for both you and your employees to complete a form—after you identify the critical competencies—and then compare and discuss the results, agreeing on a final plan that combines both views.

An alternative method is for you to complete the form and review it with your employees. This may be a more appropriate way to start if development plans have never been a part of your processes. The key here is to make sure that you keep an open mind and don't dictate what employees must do. Successful employee development requires a blend of the employee's needs and desires and those of the manager.

Whatever approach you take, communication and a good understanding of the process are critical for both you and your employees. You won't foster cooperation and full participation if employees see the process as a threat.

Selecting the right activities is essential for successful development. Developmental activities may include on-the-job, classroom/group, formal education, self-managed learning, mentoring/coaching, professional/community, and additional assessment activities. Include a variety of developmental activities depending on available resources and learning style. Some people learn best by hearing or reading, others retain the information that they see, and still others learn best by practicing or doing things. Individuals' style and preference have a big impact on their development, so keep them in mind as you pick activities. Having a discussion with your employees or reviewing your observations of past learning can be keys. Also, you may decide to try a variety of methods initially to see what works best.

When selecting developmental activities, the manager and employee should consider the availability of resources in the organization. Some activities, such as attending a training session or joining a professional organization, may involve both time and money, whereas on-the-job activities, such as delivering a presentation or facilitating a focus group session, may involve fewer resources and be just as effective.

Though knowledge is a part of any competency, just getting information through classes and webinars is not sufficient for most people to develop a competency. A good example is the SHRM competency Communication, which has a subcompetency of Listening. An employee who learns the technique of active listening and practices it is not fully competent in the skill unless he or she knows when and how to use it in a business situation. For this reason, competency development requires opportunities to use knowledge, skills, and experience in real-world situations. This is where judgment is developed.

Each of the next three chapters focuses on a particular Behavioral Cluster, covering its competencies and their definitions, as well as each competency's list of subcompetencies. Subcompetencies break down the competency so that you can target specific needs. For example, your employee may have solid written and verbal abilities but may lack presentation skills. To be at a high level in the Communication competency, all three skills are needed. Consider the subcompetencies as you select developmental activities for your employees. Next, each chapter contains descriptions of suggested developmental activities, broken down in terms of types. Also listed are suggested assessment tools for checking progress or guiding employees in areas of study.

Chapter 8 provides some basic ideas to assist with development of HR Expertise—the Technical Competencies.

Activities are described as though the person reading them is addressed. This way you can just copy the suggestions and give them to your employees.

CHAPTER 5.

Interpersonal Competencies Cluster

The Interpersonal Competencies Cluster includes Communication, Global and Cultural Effectiveness, and Relationship Management.

Communication

Definition: The KSAOs needed to effectively craft and deliver concise and informative communications, to listen to and address the concerns of others, and to transfer and translate information from one level or unit of the organization to another.

Subcompetencies:

- **Delivering messages.** Develops and delivers, to a variety of audiences, communications that are clear, persuasive, and appropriate to the topic and situation.
- **Exchanging organizational information.** Effectively translates and communicates messages among organizational levels or units.
- **Listening.** Understands information provided by others.

TABLE 5.1: COMMUNICATION COMPETENCY DEVELOPMENTAL ACTIVITIES

TYPE OF ACTIVITY	DETAILS
On the job	• Ask your boss and co-workers what information they would like to receive regularly from you, and then tell them what you'd like to hear from them. • Ask your employees what information they would like to receive regularly from you, and then tell them what you'd like to hear from them. • Before making a formal presentation, practice in front of peers. Solicit feedback, and incorporate it into the presentation. • Create and deliver a visual presentation that communicates the vision for the HR team or the organization related to your job. • Lead a team meeting. • Pay attention to the nonverbal cues of others, try to determine what emotions they are communicating, and check your understanding with them by asking before making assumptions. • Seek opportunities to speak in front of groups (for example, at business meetings, by giving presentations). • Summarize notes from meetings. Distribute the summaries to others, and ask for feedback. • Write a speech or draft an e-mail for someone in a higher leadership role in the organization. • Write an article for the department or organization; have a skilled writer or your manager review it and give suggestions for improvement.
Group classes, workshops, conferences	American Management Association programs, www.amanet.org Dale Carnegie classes, www.dalecarnegie.com/events/dale_carnegie_course Training subscription services like BizLibrary, www.bizlibrary.com Related professional association and local chapter classes and conferences, including: • Association for Talent Development (ATD), www.td.org • American Payroll Association (APA), www.americanpayroll.org • International Society of Certified Employee Benefit Specialists (ISCEBS), www.iscebs.org SHRM conferences, workshops, virtual events, and online programs: • Visit www.shrm.org/events to learn more about SHRM conferences and events. • Visit www.shrm.org/learningandcareer/learning/pages/seminars.aspx for more information about SHRM seminars. Formal education: college courses at local community and four-year colleges (usually tuition-based) Online free college courses through OpenCourseWare, for example: • MIT, https://ocw.mit.edu/index.htm • University of Utah, http://ocw.usu.edu Company/organization communication skills training: A resource for managers to develop a course is Communication Skills Training, a part of the ATD Workshop Series), https://www.td.org/Publications/Books/Communication-Skills-Training-2 Course topics might include: • Business writing. • Grammar. • Technical writing. • Communication boot camp for communicating across generations. • Communicating up, down, and across the organization. • Critical conversations. • Presentation skills. • Negotiation. The Perdue Online Writing Lab offers guidance on writing skills that can be used to provide instruction, https://owl.english.purdue.edu

CONTINUED ON NEXT PAGE

TABLE 5.1: COMMUNICATION COMPETENCY DEVELOPMENTAL ACTIVITIES CONTINUED

TYPE OF ACTIVITY	DETAILS
Self-driven activities (for example, books, articles, job shadowing, microlearning)	Read articles in professional/technical journals. Summarize the information or write a critique. As you read, look up unfamiliar words in the dictionary and use them regularly. Carefully watch recognized speakers on television, radio, and other media. Incorporate a few of those skills into your presentations. Listen to an HR book on CD, and write a summary of the book or discuss the main ideas with others. Shadow a recognized high-level communicator in the organization, and capture his or her techniques for effective communication. Take a microlearning course on communication; possible resources include Degreed (www.degreed.com) or Pathgather (www.pathgather.com). Books: • *Perfect Phrases for Documenting Employee Performance Problems*, Anne Bruce, McGraw-Hill Education, 2005. • *Crucial Conversations: Tools for Talking When Stakes Are High*, Kerry Patterson, Joseph Grenny, Ron McMillan, and Al Switzler, McGraw-Hill Education, 2011. • *Up, Down, and Sideways: High-Impact Verbal Communication for HR Professionals*, Patricia M. Buhler, SPHR, and Joel D. Worden, SHRM, 2013. • *HBR Guide to Persuasive Presentations* (Harvard Business Review Guides), Nancy Duarte, Harvard Business Review Press, 2012. • SHRM How-to Guides related to communication in HR, www.shrm.org/resourcesandtools/tools-and-samples/how-to-guides/pages/default.aspx SHRM resources: • Visit www.shrm.org/hr-today/trends-and-forecasting/special-reports-and-expert-views to read what thought leaders are saying about how to be successful in HR. • Visit community.shrm.org/home to network online with other professionals in HR using the SHRM Connect platform.
Professional/ community activities (external involvement)	• Write an article or technical report related to your field, and submit it for publication. • Speak at a local school or to members of a professional and/or community organization about what you do or a topic of interest. • Join Toastmasters International, www.toastmasters.org. • Teach a communication skills course at a local college. • Meet with a group of HR professionals internally or externally and discuss HR articles or books.
Mentoring/coaching (self and others)	• Tutor a student in reading and comprehension. • Ask a colleague or manager to observe and critique your listening skills when you interact with others, and focus on improving any deficiencies. • Identify someone in your organization who is a great presenter or communicator. Ask the person to work with you to develop your communications skills.
Assessments (focused on specific competency or subcompetency)	• Sites like Mind Tools offer inexpensive self-evaluation tools, see the article "How Good Are Your Communication Skills?," www.mindtools.com/pages/article/newCS_99.htm • The RBL Group assessments, www.rbl.net • DiSC and Myers-Briggs assessments give you feedback on personality, which can help when determining communication styles. • Professional assessment tools that target verbal skill and verbal reasoning, like the Profiles International ProfileXT, www.profilesinternational.com • SHRM Competency Diagnostic Tools, www.shrm.org/LearningAndCareer/competency-model/pages/competency-diagnostic-tools.aspx

Global and Cultural Effectiveness

Definition: The KSAOs needed to value and consider the perspectives and backgrounds of all parties, to interact with others in a global context, and to promote a diverse and inclusive workplace.

> **Subcompetencies**:
> - **Operating in a diverse workplace.** Demonstrates openness and tolerance when working with people from different cultural traditions.
> - **Operating in a global environment.** Effectively manages globally influenced workplace requirements to achieve organizational goals.
> - **Advocating for a diverse and inclusive workplace.** Designs, implements, and promotes organizational policies and practices to ensure diversity and inclusion in the workplace.

TABLE 5.2: GLOBAL AND CULTURAL EFFECTIVENESS COMPETENCY DEVELOPMENT ACTIVITIES

TYPE OF ACTIVITY	DETAILS
On the job	• Ask for feedback on your work from people you do not work with directly, particularly people who think differently from you. • Take leadership by including diverse groups when you are involved in solving problems or making changes at work. • Research diversity topics (for example, using TV specials, articles, blogs, theater), and discuss them with your co-workers. • Be alert to differing ideas, and speak up for individuals whose views you observe are not being respected. • Seek out someone from a different department, division, career, or background and spend time with that person. • Participate in a cross-functional group that reviews the organization's policies and practices related to diversity and inclusiveness. • When making decisions about hiring, promotion, and termination, examine the data to ensure an unbiased approach. • Participate in a team/task group that focuses on customers outside your location, maybe across the country or the world. • Research organizations that can provide resources/networks with diverse communities in your organization's field, like the National Society of Black Engineers (www.nsbe.org/home.aspx) or the Association of Latino Professionals for America (www.alpfa.org). • Check out the Diversity Best Practices website for a list of organizations serving women, www.diversitybestpractices.com/news-articles/20-womens-organizations-you-need-know. • Consider using crowd-sourced solutions for issues that arise related to diversity at work via HR professional networks like SHRM's Member2Member Solutions (www.shrm.org/resourcesandtools/tools-and-samples/member2member/pages/default.aspx), SHRM Connect, or LinkedIn groups. • Ask a manager from a non-HR work area to allow you to shadow him or her or one of his or her workers.
Group classes, workshops, conferences	Take college courses on different cultures, including history, languages, traditions, and communication. Check the College Board site for a list of accredited schools that offer courses in international business or studies: https://bigfuture.collegeboard.org/majors/business-international-business. SHRM conferences, workshops, virtual events, and online programs: • Visit www.shrm.org/events to learn more about SHRM conferences and events. • Visit www.shrm.org/learningandcareer/learning/pages/seminars.aspx for more information about SHRM seminars. Explore programs of the Society for Diversity, www.societyfordiversity.org. Seek a diversity certification; see Institute for Diversity Certification, www.diversitycertification.org. Learn another language focusing on current or future business or on employee opportunities using programs like Rosetta Stone, www.rosettastone.com. Take a microlearning course on global business topics. Possible resources include Degreed (www.degreed.com) or Pathgather (www.pathgather.com).

CONTINUED ON NEXT PAGE

TABLE 5.2: GLOBAL AND CULTURAL EFFECTIVENESS COMPETENCY DEVELOPMENTAL ACTIVITIES CONTINUED

TYPE OF ACTIVITY	DETAILS
Self-driven activities (for example, books, articles, job shadowing, microlearning)	• Read articles on diversity and/or global business, and write a brief description of how they might apply to your job/organization. • Research videos, books, and articles on diversity and culture, and start a discussion on how understanding these topics could help your organization be more successful. • Use the Internet to research other cultures by reading news from different parts of the world. • Establish a social media connection with someone in another country where your organization does (or might do) business. • Check out sites like the Culturosity Group LLC for resources on other cultures: www.culturosity.com/index.html. Books: • *Transformational Diversity: Why and How Intercultural Competencies Can Help Organizations to Survive and Thrive*, Fiona Citkin and Lynda Spielman, SHRM, 2011. • *Kiss, Bow, or Shake Hands: The Bestselling Guide to Doing Business in More Than 60 Countries*, Terri Morrison and Wayne A. Conaway, Adams Media, 2006. • *Making Diversity Work: 7 Steps for Defeating Bias in the Workplace*, Sondra Thiederman, Kaplan Business, 2003. Use SHRM resources and tools, including: • Diversity Tools, www.shrm.org/resourcesandtools/hr-topics/pages/diversity-and-inclusion.aspx • Global HR, www.shrm.org/resourcesandtools/hr-topics/global-hr/pages/default.aspx • Visit www.shrm.org/hr-today/trends-and-forecasting/special-reports-and-expert-views to read what thought leaders are saying about how to be successful in HR. • Visit community.shrm.org/home to network online with other professionals in HR using the SHRM Connect platform.
Professional/ community activities (external involvement)	• Join a social organization focused on an ethnic group you do not know much about. • Volunteer for a nonprofit organization that assists immigrants. • Get involved with organizations that focus on inclusion and diversity, like the National Diversity Council, www.nationaldiversitycouncil.org. • Join the board of a nonprofit that assists racial, social, ethnic, or gender groups you do not know a lot about but that can benefit from your HR knowledge.
Mentoring/coaching (self and others)	• Find a coach or mentor who has a different background from you. • Mentor or coach someone from a different age group. • Work with a business professional who is of a different gender to gain perspectives on how to deal with employees of that gender. • Join an organization dedicated to mentoring, like the National Mentoring Partnership, www.mentoring.org. • Participate in the Harvard Mentoring Project, https://sites.sph.harvard.edu/wmy.
Assessments (focused on specific competency or subcompetency)	• Myers-Briggs and DiSC provide information that can lead to understanding individual differences among people. • Participate in Harvard's Project Implicit to determine your own unconscious biases, https://implicit.harvard.edu/implicit/aboutus.html. • Professional assessment tools that provide behavioral information, like the Profiles International ProfileXT, www.profilesinternational.com. • The RBL Group assessments, www.rbl.net. • *Diversity Awareness Profile*, Karen Stinson, Wiley, 2007. • SHRM Competency Diagnostic Tools, www.shrm.org/LearningAndCareer/competency-model/pages/competency-diagnostic-tools.aspx

Relationship Management

Definition: The KSAOs needed to create and maintain a network of professional contacts inside and outside the organization, to build and maintain relationships, to work as an effective member of a team, and to manage conflict while supporting the organization.

Subcompetencies:

- **Networking.** Effectively builds a network of professional contacts both inside and outside the organization.
- **Relationship building.** Effectively builds and maintains relationships both inside and outside the organization.
- **Teamwork.** Participates as an effective team member, and builds, promotes, and leads effective teams.
- **Conflict management.** Manages and resolves conflicts by identifying areas of common interest among the parties in conflict.
- **Negotiation.** Reaches mutually acceptable agreements with negotiating parties inside and outside the organization.

TABLE 5.3: RELATIONSHIP MANAGEMENT COMPETENCY DEVELOPMENTAL ACTIVITIES

TYPE OF ACTIVITY	DETAILS
On the job	• Think about work relationships that you have had, and select a successful one and one that is/was not successful; then analyze them by making a list of words that describe each to determine the best practices/aspects to use going forward. • Ask a peer or manager to describe his or her experiences in working with you, including what is good and what is not. • Participate on projects that need cross-functional teamwork. • Volunteer to help at least one person in your work unit or department each week/month. • Volunteer to facilitate a discussion with others to solve a work problem. • Meet with individuals from other areas of the company, and ask how you or your employees can work together more effectively; then decide how you can use their suggestions. • Ask people who do not normally work together to work on a problem or project together. • Identify an organizational problem or challenge, and then work with a group to come up with a solution that you then pitch to management; ask for feedback on your presentation to management, whether you are successful or not. • Pass along interesting articles or blogs to others who might benefit from the information. • Consider what changes might be made to HR policies to help build a better relationship with employees while protecting business interests.
Group classes, workshops, conferences	Dale Carnegie courses, www.dalecarnegie.com Disney's Professional Development list, Disney's Approach to Employee Engagement, https://disneyinstitute.com/courses SHRM conferences, workshops, virtual events, and online programs: • Visit www.shrm.org/events to learn more about SHRM conferences and events. • Visit www.shrm.org/learningandcareer/learning/pages/seminars.aspx for more information about SHRM seminars. Business Relationship Management Institute also offers certification courses, https://brm.institute/professional-development/business-relationship-management-professional-brmp. Franklin Covey courses, www.franklincovey.com College courses on any of the subcompetencies listed above

CONTINUED ON NEXT PAGE

TABLE 5.3: RELATIONSHIP MANAGEMENT COMPETENCY DEVELOPMENTAL ACTIVITIES CONTINUED

TYPE OF ACTIVITY	DETAILS
Self-driven activities (for example, books, articles, job shadowing, microlearning)	Books: • *What Color Is Your Brain?*, Sheila N. Glazov, Slack Incorporated, 2007. • *The Emotional Intelligence Quick Book: Everything You Need to Know to Put Your EQ to Work*, Travis Bradberry and Jean Greaves, Fireside, 2005. • *The Speed of Trust: The One Thing That Changes Everything,* Steven Covey, Free Press, 2006. • *All for One: 10 Strategies for Building Trusted Client Partnerships,* Andrew Sobel, Wiley, 2009. • *How to Win Friends and Influence People*, Dale Carnegie, 2006. • *Performing Under Pressure: The Science of Doing Your Best When It Matters Most,* Hendrie Weisinger and J. P. Pawliw-Fry, Crown Business, 2015. • *Nine Minutes on Monday: The Quick and Easy Way to Turn Managers into Leaders,* James Robbins, McGraw-Hill, 2012. • *Reality-Based Leadership: Ditch the Drama, Restore Sanity to the Workplace, and Turn Excuses into Results,* Cy Wakeman and Larry Winget, Wiley, 2010. Visit www.mindtools.com for tools to build relationships and collaboration. SHRM resources: • Visit www.shrm.org/hr-today/trends-and-forecasting/special-reports-and-expert-views to read what thought leaders are saying about how to be successful in HR. • Visit community.shrm.org/home to network online with other professionals in HR using the SHRM Connect platform.
Professional/community activities (external involvement)	• Work on enhancing your professional network by attending non-HR meetings and events to meet people outside your normal sphere. • Network by introducing yourself and then asking people about themselves before telling them about you; listen carefully before speaking. • Volunteer to work on community projects at organizations that do good (for example, Habitat for Humanity) where you might be exposed to people outside your normal sphere—use the experience to get to know more about them.
Mentoring/ coaching (self and others)	• Find a mentor who is recognized as someone who works well with leaders and employees in the organization, and ask him or her to work with you to develop your skills. • Seek out someone in a different industry or field, and ask him or her to coach you on how to build networks and relationships in that area. • Communicate with a less experienced professional in a different generational group, and meet regularly to discuss how you see trends and activities within the company to better understand each other.
Assessments (focused on specific competency or subcompetency)	• SHRM Competency Diagnostic Tools, www.shrm.org/LearningAndCareer/competency-model/pages/competency-diagnostic-tools.aspx • Myers-Briggs Type Indicator • The RBL Group assessments, www.rbl.net • To further understand how you react to and interact with others, visit the website of Sheila Glazov, author of *What Color Is Your Brain?*, www.sheilaglazov.com/brain-quizzes. • Check your emotional intelligence on the Institute for Health and Human Potential site, www.ihhp.com/free-eq-quiz.

CHAPTER 6.

Business Competencies Cluster

The Business Competencies Cluster includes Business Acumen, Consultation, and Critical Evaluation.

Business Acumen

Definition: The KSAOs needed to understand the organization's operations, functions, and external environment and to apply business tools and analyses that inform HR initiatives and operations consistent with the overall strategic direction of the organization.

 Subcompetencies:
- **Business and competitive awareness.** Understands the organization's operations, functions, products, and services, as well as the competitive, economic, social, and political environments in which the organization operates.
- **Business analysis.** Applies business metrics, principles, and technologies to inform and address business needs.
- **Strategic alignment.** Aligns HR strategy, communications, initiatives, and operations with the organization's strategic direction.

TABLE 6.1: BUSINESS ACUMEN COMPETENCY DEVELOPMENTAL ACTIVITIES

TYPE OF ACTIVITY	DETAILS
On the job	• Attend management meetings that discuss business planning and take notes; after the meeting, ask business leaders questions to gain understanding of business issues. • Help your employees or co-workers understand how what they do affects the bottom line and success for the organization. • Learn about business results and what you can do to impact them. • Set individual or department goals that are clearly aligned with organization strategic and business goals. • Schedule meetings with managers in other departments to ask them about what the department does and how HR can support their goals. • Volunteer to be on company task groups to solve a significant business problem. • Work with the recruiting function or IT to research, plan, and initiate campaigns using social media—including augmented reality and video branding—to recruit new employees. • Start a business book discussion group with employees from across the organization. • Participate in a temporary assignment in a department or workgroup outside HR. • Research your industry's trends, and evaluate how they will affect your business going forward; share your thoughts with managers outside HR, and ask for their thoughts. • Focus on presenting ideas and solutions from a business versus HR perspective—for example results and return on investment versus nice or kind; connection between employee behavior and business success.
Group classes, workshops, conferences	Formal degrees in business or business subjects are offered by many colleges and universities. American Management Association courses, www.amanet.org/training/ama-seminars.aspx SHRM conferences, workshops, virtual events and online programs: • Visit www.shrm.org/events to learn more about SHRM conferences and events. • Visit www.shrm.org/learningandcareer/learning/pages/seminars.aspx for more information about SHRM seminars. Finance and accounting: Explore courses designed for nonfinancial managers. Examples include: • Stanford University, www.gsb.stanford.edu/exec-ed/programs/finance-accounting-non-financial-executive • The Wharton School, www.executiveeducation.wharton.upenn.edu/for-individuals/all-programs/finance-and-accounting-for-the-non-financial-manager Consider a certificate in financial management versus a degree—many colleges offer these programs. Sales and marketing: American Marketing Association courses, www.ama.org. Check out free online marketing courses listed by WordStream, www.wordstream.com/blog/ws/2014/08/19/free-online-marketing-courses. Technology: check out companies like Decoded that help nontechnical managers understand technology, www.decoded.com. Business operations/logistics: APICS, www.apics.org Government and regulatory: SHRM and other industry conferences Metrics/analytics/business indicators: online courses like those that Duke University offers, https://online.duke.edu/projects/business-metrics-for-data-driven-companies

CONTINUED ON NEXT PAGE

TABLE 6.1: BUSINESS ACUMEN COMPETENCY DEVELOPMENTAL ACTIVITIES CONTINUED

TYPE OF ACTIVITY	DETAILS
Self-driven activities (for example, books, articles, job shadowing, microlearning)	Books: • *Developing Business Acumen,* Jennifer Currence, SHRM, 2016. • *Business-Focused HR: 11 Processes to Drive Results,* Shane S. Douthitt and Scott P. Mondore, SHRM, 2011. • *Becoming the Evidence-Based Manager: Making the Science of Management Work for You,* Gary Latham, Nicholas Brealey, 2011. • *Leading Your Business Forward: Aligning Goals, People, and Systems for Sustainable Success,* John Pyecha, Shane Yount, Seth Davies, and Anna Versteeg, McGraw-Hill, 2013. • *Cracking the IT Code: Technology Management for Non-Technology Managers,* Anthony L Butler, Indie Books International, 2015. • *Predictive Analytics: The Power to Predict Who Will Click, Buy, Lie, or Die,* Eric Siegel, Wiley, 2013. • *Business Literacy Survival Guide for HR Professionals,* Regan W. Garey, SHRM, 2011. • *HBR's 10 Must Reads 2016: The Definitive Management Ideas of the Year from Harvard Business Review,* Harvard Business Review Press, 2016. Look for magazines in areas related to your business or industry, www.freetrademagazines.com. Listen to TED Talks on various business subjects. Attend seminars and lectures outside of the organization. Participate in external forums that discuss current government issues and future trends. Think about how this information affects your work. SHRM resources: • Visit www.shrm.org/hr-today/trends-and-forecasting/special-reports-and-expert-views to read what thought leaders are saying about how to be successful in HR. • Visit community.shrm.org/home to network online with other professionals in HR using the SHRM Connect platform.
Professional/ community activities (external involvement)	• Join or attend Chamber of Commerce or other business group events and meetings. • Volunteer or join the board of a nonprofit to contribute business knowledge and to learn from other business volunteers. • Join and participate in small-business groups on social media sites like LinkedIn and SHRM Connect. • Volunteer to assist with student chapters of various business and HR organizations; Rasmussen College offers a list of organizations in accounting, finance, marketing, business management, supply chain management, and HR (www.rasmussen.edu/degrees/business/blog/top-professional-associations-for-business-students). Government and regulatory: • Participate in SHRM Government Affairs activities and with organizations that are involved in government affairs for your organization's industry.
Mentoring/ coaching (self and others)	• Evaluate your weakest area in business, and seek a mentor or coach who is an expert in that area. • Pick your strongest area of business knowledge, and volunteer to coach someone in that discipline. • Become a volunteer judge or advisor for DECA: DECA student members have the opportunity to network with local business leaders and develop business skills through mock presentations and competitions, www.deca.org
Assessments (focused on specific competency or subcompetency)	• SHRM Competency Diagnostic Tools, www.shrm.org/LearningAndCareer/competency-model/pages/competency-diagnostic-tools.aspx • Contact assessment centers for specific business area aptitude tests. • The RBL Group assessments, www.rbl.net

Consultation

Definition: The KSAOs needed to work with organizational stakeholders in evaluating business challenges and identifying opportunities for the design, implementation, and evaluation of change initiatives and to build ongoing support for HR solutions that meet the changing needs of customers and the business.

Subcompetencies:

- **Evaluating business challenges.** Works with business partners and leaders to identify business challenges and opportunities for HR solutions.
- **Designing HR solutions.** Works with business partners and leaders to design HR solutions and initiatives that meet business needs.
- **Implementing and supporting HR solutions.** Works with business partners and leaders to implement and support HR solutions and initiatives.
- **Change management.** Leads and supports maintenance of or changes in strategy, organization, and/or operations.
- **Customer interaction.** Provides high-quality customer service and contributes to a strong customer service culture.

TABLE 6.2: CONSULTATION COMPETENCY DEVELOPMENTAL ACTIVITIES

TYPE OF ACTIVITY	DETAILS
On the job	• Identify a peer leader with a history of promotions within his or her team. Meet with this person to discuss how he or she prepares team members for promotional opportunities. • Keep a log of each commitment that you make. Review the promises that you made and whether you followed through on them and why. Devise a plan to work on specific issues. • Participate on a project team, and volunteer to co-lead the project with an experienced project manager. • Work with others in your department to come up with solutions to organizational problems using creative approaches. • Ask your manager to increase the scope of your decision-making authority. • Identify someone who is successful at solving problems, and ask if you can think through a problem with him or her to enhance your problem-solving skills. • Research a significant problem in your department, examine the background, and break it down. Develop a plan to solve it, and consider possible pitfalls. Ask someone good at problem-solving to discuss your solution. • Think about an area that you have strong emotions about at work, and develop a list of logical ways to deal with it. • Practice listening, asking questions, and analyzing before offering solutions. • Consider how the culture of a particular department or group influences the behaviors in that group before suggesting solutions/ideas. • Each week commit to doing something different (for example, spend time with someone from a different background, listen to different music, take a different route home). • When presented with a new idea, ask people to first identify and discuss what they like, rather than what they dislike, about an idea. • Use reliable social media (LinkedIn, SHRM's Member2Member Solutions, other business networks) to crowd-source answers to problems to be exposed to ideas other than your own.

CONTINUED ON NEXT PAGE

TABLE 6.2: CONSULTATION COMPETENCY DEVELOPMENTAL ACTIVITIES CONTINUED

TYPE OF ACTIVITY	DETAILS
Group classes, workshops, conferences	College courses that include: • Project management • Coaching • Creativity • Analytical reasoning Project management certificate programs like Katz Business School, University of Pittsburgh, www.business.pitt.edu/katz/mba/academics/certificates/project-management.php Formal project management certifications: • Project Management Institute (PMI), Project Management Professional or other certifications, www.pmi.org/certifications • CompTIA Project+ http://certification.comptia.org/getCertified/certifications/project.aspx Online programs, for example: • Business Problem Solving, New Horizons Computer Learning Center, https://nhlearningsolutions.com/FindTraining/CourseOutline/tabid/436/Default.aspx?courseID=200000352 Courses on various subjects through Coursera: • Effective Problem-Solving and Decision-Making, University of California, Irvine, www.coursera.org/learn/problem-solving • Creativity, Innovation, and Change, The Pennsylvania State University, www.coursera.org/learn/creativity-innovation Free courses listed through Creative Boom, www.creativeboom.com/resources/50-free-online-courses-for-creatives-and-entrepreneurs Scrum Alliance events, www.scrumalliance.org/courses-events/events/global-gatherings/2016/orlando-2016 The Mentoring Institute (the University of New Mexico) conference, http://mentor.unm.edu/conference SHRM Conferences, workshops, virtual events, and online programs: • Visit www.shrm.org/events to learn more about SHRM conferences and events. • Visit www.shrm.org/learningandcareer/learning for more information about SHRM seminars.
Self-driven activities (for example, books, articles, job shadowing, microlearning)	Books: • *Step-by-Step Problem Solving: A Practical Guide to Ensure Problems Get (and Stay) Solved*, Richard Chang and Keith Kelly, Practical Learning Press, 1993. • *Think Again: Why Good Leaders Make Bad Decisions and How to Keep It from Happening to You,* Sydney Finkelstein, Andrew Campbell, and Jo Whitehead, Harvard Business Press, 2009. • *The Data Squad: Building People Analytics Capabilities Research,* Jenna Filipkowski, Human Capital Institute, 2016. • *Making Things Happen: Mastering Project Management (Theory in Practice),* Scott Berkun, O'Reilly Media, 2008. • *Essentials of Project Management,* Wendy Bliss, SHRM/Harvard Business School Press, 2006. • *Common Sense Talent Management: Using Strategic Human Resources to Improve Company Performance,* Steven T. Hunt, Pfeiffer, 2014. • *Manager's Guide to Effective Coaching,* Marshall J. Cook and Laura Poole, McGraw-Hill, 2011. Identify someone in your organization who delegates responsibility well, and meet with him or her or shadow the person for a day. Take a short course in innovation management through the ShortCoursesPortal, www.shortcoursesportal.com/disciplines/240/innovation-management.html. Play games that increase problem-solving skills (for example, bridge, Bid Whist, Spades, Risk). SHRM resources: • Visit www.shrm.org/hr-today/trends-and-forecasting/special-reports-and-expert-views to read what thought leaders are saying about how to be successful in HR. • Visit community.shrm.org/home to network online with other professionals in HR using the SHRM Connect platform.

CONTINUED ON NEXT PAGE

TABLE 6.2: CONSULTATION COMPETENCY DEVELOPMENTAL ACTIVITIES CONTINUED

TYPE OF ACTIVITY	DETAILS
Professional/ community activities (external involvement)	• Join and participate in the International Coach Federation (consider attending meetings of local chapters), www.coachfederation.org. • Join and participate in the Project Management Institute, www.pmi.org. • Volunteer to do projects and solve problems for nonprofits or small businesses through organizations looking for professional assistance like BVU: The Center for Nonprofit Excellence, www.bvuvolunteers.org/ or The National Council of Nonprofits, www.councilofnonprofits.org/tools-resources/volunteers as well as doing an on-line search for local organizations. • Join the Mentoring Institute, http://mentor.unm.edu.
Mentoring/coaching (self and others)	• Seek out a mentor who is a professional consultant in HR or a related business, and ask him or her to help you develop your skills. • Join or follow the Human Capital Institute to learn and practice better coaching and mentoring, www.hci.org/talent-management/learning-development/coaching-and-mentoring. • Volunteer to coach a student or lower-level employee in an area in which you possess some expertise to further develop your coaching skills.
Assessments (focused on specific competency or subcompetency)	• SHRM Competency Diagnostic Tools, www.shrm.org/LearningAndCareer/competency-model/pages/competency-diagnostic-tools.aspx • The RBL Group assessments, www.rbl.net • Assess personality tests, http://product.assess-systems.com/assess • Simple assessment for creativity, www.kellogg.northwestern.edu/faculty/uzzi/ftp/page176.html • Check with assessment centers for other tests/assessments.

Critical Evaluation

Definition: The KSAOs needed to collect and analyze qualitative and quantitative data and to interpret and promote findings that evaluate HR initiatives and inform business decisions and recommendations.

Subcompetencies:

- **Data advocate.** Understands and promotes the importance and utility of data.
- **Data gathering.** Understands how to determine data utility and identifies and gathers data to inform organizational decisions.
- **Data analysis.** Analyzes data to evaluate HR initiatives and business challenges.
- **Evidence-based decision-making.** Uses the results of data analysis to inform the best course of action.

TABLE 6.3: CRITICAL EVALUATION COMPETENCY DEVELOPMENTAL ACTIVITIES

TYPE OF ACTIVITY	DETAILS
On the job	• Research the use of new technologies in HR, and determine how you can use them in your situation. Present your thoughts to your manager. • Listen to other people's opinions and suggestions. List all positive aspects; then take a more critical view. • When approaching any situation, practice asking *why, where, what, who, when*, and *how*. • Control gut reactions by writing down your first thought and then considering other alternatives. • When making a decision, consider all the alternatives and come up with three possible solutions. Discuss them with stakeholders. • Practice identifying and challenging the assumptions and beliefs that underlie your thinking, conclusions, and decisions. • Determine the root cause of problems; then come up with the costs of not solving them and the impacts if they are corrected. • Keep track each time you collect information before making a decision, and compare the results and the relationship with data collection. • Seek out subject matter experts when working on projects and problems. • Make sure you can thoroughly explain your research and decisions. • Back up your decisions with well-defined data.
Group classes, workshops, conferences	SHRM courses and seminars, for example: • Critical Evaluation: Building HR Metrics to Guide Decisions, https://store.shrm.org/s-hr-metrics.html SHRM conferences, workshops, virtual events, and online programs: • Visit www.shrm.org/events to learn more about SHRM conferences and events. • Visit www.shrm.org/learningandcareer/learning/pages/seminars.aspx for more information about SHRM seminars. Courses from Think Watson, www.thinkwatson.com College courses in critical thinking, problem-solving, and research methods

CONTINUED ON NEXT PAGE

TABLE 6.3: CRITICAL EVALUATION COMPETENCY DEVELOPMENTAL ACTIVITIES CONTINUED

TYPE OF ACTIVITY	DETAILS
Self-driven activities (for example, books, articles, job shadowing, microlearning)	Books: • *Asking the Right Questions: A Guide to Critical Thinking* by Neil Browne and Stuart Keeley, Prentice Hall, 2009. • *Think Again: Why Good Leaders Make Bad Decisions and How to Keep It from Happening to You* by Sydney Finkelstein, Jo Whitehead, and Andrew Campbell, Harvard Business Press, 2009. • *Critical Thinking: Proven Strategies to Improve Decision Making Skills, Increase Intuition and Think Smarter,* Simon Bradley and Nicole Price, CreateSpace, 2016. • *Think Smarter: Critical Thinking to Improve Problem-Solving and Decision-Making Skills,* Michael Kallet, Wiley, 2014. • *Critical Thinking: Your Ultimate Critical Thinking Guide: Effective Strategies That Will Make You Improve Critical Thinking and Decision Making Skills,* Gerard Johnson, CreateSpace, 2016. • *Applying Advanced Analytics to HR Management Decisions: Methods for Selection, Developing Incentives, and Improving Collaboration,* James C. Sesil, FT Press, 2013. • *Business Research Methods,* William G. Zikmund, Barry J. Babin, Jon C. Carr, and Mitch Griffin, South-Western and Cengage Learning, 2012. Articles: "How to Train Your Mind to Think Critically and Form Your Own Opinions," Thorin Klosowski, *Lifehacker* (blog), February 6, 2014, http://lifehacker.com/how-to-train-your-mind-to-think-critically-and-form-you-1516998286. "Critical Thinking Skills: What Are They and How Do I Get Them?," Winston Sieck, November 5, 2015, http://thinkeracademy.com/critical-thinking-skills. Information on the Free Management Library website, http://managementhelp.org/businessresearch SHRM resources: • Visit www.shrm.org/hr-today/trends-and-forecasting/special-reports-and-expert-views to read what thought leaders are saying about how to be successful in HR. • Visit community.shrm.org/home to network online with other professionals in HR using the SHRM Connect platform.
Professional/ community activities (external involvement)	• Become involved in or follow organizations that support and research critical thinking, like the Foundation for Critical Thinking, www.criticalthinking.org. • Get certified in critical thinking: Critical Thinking Foundation, "Become Certified in the Paul-Elder Framework for Critical Thinking," February 2016, www.criticalthinking.org/data/certification-white-paper.pdf.
Mentoring/ coaching (self and others)	• Seek out a mentor or coach who frequently sees things differently than you do, and ask him or her for feedback on your actions and decisions. • Become a mentor to someone who thinks differently than you do.
Assessments (focused on specific competency or subcompetency)	• SHRM Competency Diagnostic Tools, www.shrm.org/LearningAndCareer/competency-model/pages/competency-diagnostic-tools.aspx • The RBL Group assessments, www.rbl.net • Watson-Glaser Critical Thinking Appraisal, www.thinkwatson.com/assessments/watson-glaser • Profiles International ProfileXT instrument, aspects related to decision-making, www.profilesinternational.com

CHAPTER 7.

Leadership Competencies Cluster

The Leadership Competencies Cluster includes Ethical Practice and Leadership and Navigation.

Ethical Practice

Definition: The KSAOs needed to maintain high levels of personal and professional integrity, and to act as an ethical agent who promotes core values, integrity and accountability throughout the organization.

Subcompetencies:

- **Personal integrity.** Demonstrates high levels of integrity in personal relationships and behaviors.
- **Professional integrity.** Demonstrates high levels of integrity in professional relationships and behaviors.
- **Ethical agent.** Cultivates the organization's ethical environment and ensures that policies and practices reflect ethical values.

TABLE 7.1: ETHICAL PRACTICE COMPETENCY DEVELOPMENTAL ACTIVITIES

TYPE OF ACTIVITY	DETAILS
On the job	• Create a personal set of guiding principles for handling confidential information. • Find an executive whose values and principles you admire, and suggest to your manager that the person be invited to speak to your department about the value of business ethics. • Identify a trustworthy co-worker, find out what he or she does to earn trust from others, and model that behavior. • Review policies related to ethics, privacy, and confidentiality, and discuss them with co-workers. • When faced with a difficult ethical decision, ask yourself: (a) Is it legal or does it violate a company policy?, (b) Are all people involved being treated fairly?, and (c) Will I be proud of my actions? • Review codes of ethics for HR (available from SHRM) and other professions in your organization, and work to suggest a corporate code of ethics that combines the ideas. • Stand up for ethical behaviors in your daily work. • If your organization has not identified core values, volunteer to lead a team that establishes them.

CONTINUED ON NEXT PAGE

TABLE 7.1: ETHICAL PRACTICE COMPETENCY DEVELOPMENTAL ACTIVITIES CONTINUED

TYPE OF ACTIVITY	DETAILS
Group classes, workshops, conferences	SHRM conferences, workshops, virtual events, and online programs: • Visit www.shrm.org/events to learn more about SHRM conferences and events. • Visit www.shrm.org/learningandcareer/learning/pages/seminars.aspx for more information about SHRM seminars. College courses in workplace ethics: • Master of Science in Business Ethics and Compliance, New England College of Business and Ethics, https://www.necb.edu/masters-degrees/master-of-science-in-business-ethics-and-compliance • GradSchools.com provides descriptions to other programs, www.gradschools.com/programs/philosophy-ethics/ethics ShortCoursesPortal, www.shortcoursesportal.com/studies/61750/business-ethics-and-corporate-responsibility.html CSR Training Institute, www.csrtraininginstitute.com
Self-driven activities (for example, books, articles, job shadowing, microlearning)	Books: • *The Fissured Workplace: Why Work Became So Bad for So Many and What Can Be Done to Improve It*, David Weil, Harvard University Press, 2014. • *Building a Culture of Distinction*, Sheila L. Margolis, Workplace Culture Institute, 2010. • *Ethics: Theory and Practice*, Jacques P. Thiroux and Keith W. Krasemann, Prentice Hall, 2008. • *Accountability: Freedom and Responsibility without Control*, Rob Lebow and Randy Spitzer, Berrett-Koehler Publishers, 2002. • *Managing Business Ethics, Straight Talk about How to Do It Right* Linda K. Trevino and Katherine A. Nelson, Wiley, 2010. • *Vision, Values, and Courage: Leadership for Quality Management*, Neil Snyder, Simon and Schuster, 2010. • Read about the Global Business Ethics Survey conducted by the Ethics and Compliance Initiative, *Global Business Ethics Survey: Measuring Risk and Promoting Workplace Integrity*, www.ethics.org/research/gbes. Articles (available at): • *Business Ethics* magazine, http://business-ethics.com • The Free Management Library, http://managementhelp.org/businessethics • *Harvard Business Review*, https://hbr.org/topic/ethics SHRM resources: • Visit www.shrm.org/hr-today/trends-and-forecasting/special-reports-and-expert-views to read what thought leaders are saying about how to be successful in HR. • Visit community.shrm.org/home to network online with other professionals in HR using the SHRM Connect platform.
Professional/community activities (external involvement)	• Get involved with the Institute for Global Ethics, www.globalethics.org. • Volunteer for a nonprofit focused on addressing an ethical or social issue that you care about, such as homelessness or domestic violence.
Mentoring/ coaching (self and others)	Ask someone who you know has successfully dealt with difficult and unpopular decisions to coach you on how to be successful in that regard.
Assessments (focused on specific competency or subcompetency)	• Hogan Development Survey, www.hoganassessments.com/assessment/hogan-development-survey/ • The RBL Group assessments, www.rbl.net • SHRM Competency Diagnostic Tools, www.shrm.org/LearningAndCareer/competency-model/pages/competency-diagnostic-tools.aspx

Leadership and Navigation

Definition: The KSAOs needed to navigate the organization and accomplish HR goals, to create a compelling vision and mission for HR that aligns with the strategic direction and culture of the organization, to lead and promote organizational change, to manage the implementation and execution of HR initiatives, and to promote the role of HR as a key business partner.

Subcompetencies:

- **Navigating the organization.** Works within the parameters of the organization's hierarchy, processes, systems, and policies.
- **Vision.** Defines and supports a coherent vision and long-term goals for HR that support the strategic direction of the organization.
- **Managing HR initiatives.** Executes the implementation and management of HR projects or initiatives that support HR and organizational objectives.
- **Influence.** Inspires colleagues to understand and pursue the strategic vision and goals of HR and the organization.

TABLE 7.2: LEADERSHIP AND NAVIGATION COMPETENCY DEVELOPMENTAL ACTIVITIES

TYPE OF ACTIVITY	DETAILS
On the job	• Build and present a business case for (or against) a merger, acquisition, joint venture, or strategic alliance. • Volunteer to participate in implementing an organizationwide process or system change. • Develop and implement a plan to cut business costs or control inventories. • Work with a team to negotiate agreements with external alliance partners or regulatory organizations. • Ask to lead in a high-pressure or high-visibility situation, such as a media relations challenge. • Research the company's business model and how it makes money. • Learn about company-specific processes and product offerings. • Study the organization's supply chain elements, application of products, markets, and economic cycles. • Ask your manager to explain organization revenues, expenses, profits, customers, and growth. • Seek subject matter experts in the organization in accounting, finance, marketing/sales, strategy, and the analysis and interpretation of financial statements, and ask them to help you learn more about these topics. • Review the company's internal ethics codes, and if none exists, research and suggest some (see, for example, the SHRM Code of Ethics www.shrm.org/about-shrm/pages/code-of-ethics.aspx). • Set goals and document results, including the learning from each activity. • Practice empowering others by delegating tasks that you usually do yourself; provide guidance, and follow up and analyze results. • Develop a network of individuals from other parts of the business who can provide information useful in developing HR processes. • Create a strategic plan for your position, team, or department that aligns with that of the organization, and discuss it with your boss and reports.
Group classes, workshops, conferences	Degrees and college courses in leadership Programs offered by the Center for Creative Leadership, www.ccl.org The Leader's Institute, www.leadersinstitute.com List of free online courses in leadership at Class Central, www.class-central.com/subject/management-and-leadership Leadership course list on AcademicCourses.com, www.academiccourses.com/Courses/Leadership SHRM conferences, workshops, virtual events and online programs: • Visit www.shrm.org/events to learn more about SHRM conferences and events. • Visit www.shrm.org/learningandcareer/learning/pages/seminars.aspx for more information about SHRM seminars.

CONTINUED ON NEXT PAGE

TABLE 7.2: LEADERSHIP AND NAVIGATION COMPETENCY DEVELOPMENTAL ACTIVITIES CONTINUED

TYPE OF ACTIVITY	DETAILS
Self-driven activities (for example, books, articles, job shadowing, microlearning)	Books: • *Developing the Leaders Around You, How to Help Others Reach Their Full Potential*, John C. Maxwell, Thomas Nelson, 2005. • *First, Break All the Rules: What the World's Greatest Managers Do Differently,* Marcus Buckingham and Curt Coffman, Simon and Schuster, 1999. • *Hidden Strengths: Unleashing the Crucial Leadership Skills You Already Have,* Milo Sindell and Thuy Sindell, Berrett-Koehler Publishers, 2015. • *HBR's 10 Must Reads on Leadership,* Harvard Business Review, Harvard Business School Press, 2011. • *The Discover Your True North Fieldbook: A Personal Guide to Finding Your Authentic Leadership,* Revised, Nick Craig, Bill George, and Scott Snook, Jossey-Bass, 2015. • *Winning the Long Game: How Strategic Leaders Shape the Future,* Steven Krupp and Paul J. H. Schoemaker, Public Affairs, 2014. • *Start with Why: How Great Leaders Inspire Everyone to Take Action,* Simon Sinek, Portfolio, 2009. • *Management and Machiavelli: An Inquiry into the Politics of Corporate Life,* Antony Jay, Holt, Rinehart & Winston, 1968. • *View from the Top: Leveraging Human and Organization Capital to Create Value,* edited by Richard L. Antoine, Elizabeth "Libby" Sartain, Dave Ulrich, and Patrick M. Wright, SHRM, 2016. • *Emotional Intelligence 2.0,* Travis Bradberry, Jean Greaves, and Patrick Lencioni, TalentSmart, 2009. • *Forget a Mentor, Find a Sponsor: The New Way to Fast-Track Your Career,* Sylvia Ann Hewlett, Harvard Business Press, 2013. • Shadow a leader in another department, take note of how he or she approaches problems, and ask to discuss what you observed. • Take advantage of microlearning related to leadership using sources such as Degreed (www.degreed.com) or Pathgather (www.pathgather.com). • Look for podcasts often offered by HR vendors for free like Ultimate Software, www.ultimatesoftware.com/Helping-Managers-Become-Better-Leaders-Podcast; keep in mind that the vendors will highlight their products. • Sign up for and read HR blogs like *HR Bartender,* www.hrbartender.com/day-job. SHRM resources: • Visit www.shrm.org/hr-today/trends-and-forecasting/special-reports-and-expert-views to read what thought leaders are saying about how to be successful in HR. • Visit community.shrm.org/home to network online with other professionals in HR using the SHRM Connect platform.
Professional/community activities (external involvement)	• Join a nonprofit board or apply to be an advisor to a small family-owned business board to observe other leaders and practice new skills. • Volunteer for leadership positions in professional organizations like SHRM at the local/chapter, state, or national level. • Investigate the activities provided by NMA, a Leadership Development Organization, https://nma1.org. • Consider the Association of Leadership Programs, which has chapters in many cities in the U.S., https://alpleaders.org/about/. • Join or participate in the National Leadership Institute, www.nationalleadershipinstitute.org.
Mentoring/coaching (self and others)	• Find a coach or mentor who has the position you aspire to in the future and ask him or her to help you develop in your areas of need to reach that goal. • Establish a personal "advisory board" of individuals who have leadership traits you aspire to, and meet with them on a regular basis providing information on your activities and asking for thoughts/feedback. • Consider finding a sponsor—a senior-level champion who believes in your potential and is willing to advocate for you as you pursue the next level (see Sylvia Ann Hewlett's book listed above)
Assessments (focused on specific competency or subcompetency)	• SHRM Competency Diagnostic Tools, www.shrm.org/LearningAndCareer/competency-model/pages/competency-diagnostic-tools.aspx • The RBL Group assessments, www.rbl.net • Center for Creative Leadership assessments, www.ccl.org/lead-it-yourself-solutions/assessments

CHAPTER 8

HR Technical Competencies

Definition: The knowledge of principles, practices, and functions of effective human resource management.

TABLE 8.1: GENERAL HR TECHNICAL COMPETENCY DEVELOPMENTAL ACTIVITIES

TYPE OF ACTIVITY	DETAILS
On the job	• Work with employees and managers to consider the effectiveness of HR processes you are responsible for. • When responding to stakeholders, make sure you listen carefully and research thoroughly before giving answers or advice. • When confronted with an HR problem, confer with another person before proceeding. • Make a list of your key stakeholders, and then talk with them to find out what they need from you. • Review all HR procedures and policies ensuring you know your role and who to go to for expertise. • Develop an understanding of workplace risk management issues, where to go for help, and with whom to confer. • Develop your knowledge of general HR practices and technology. • Track and analyze any errors that you are responsible for in HR transactions, determine how to prevent future issues, and discuss with your boss or others involved. • Stay up-to-date on relevant laws and regulations. • Learn about relevant HR technology systems for administrative and service activities. • Maintain strong networks both inside and outside so that you know what trends are occurring in your industry that will impact your workplace.

CONTINUED ON NEXT PAGE

TABLE 8.1: GENERAL HR TECHNICAL COMPETENCY DEVELOPMENTAL ACTIVITIES CONTINUED

TYPE OF ACTIVITY	DETAILS
Group classes, workshops, conferences	College courses, certificates, and degrees in HR SHRM's HR Program Directory lists HR programs that include HR- and HR-related degree programs that align with SHRM's recommended guidelines for HR education at the undergraduate and graduate level: www.shrm.org/academicinitiatives/students/pages/hrprogramdirectory.aspx. ShortCoursesPortal, www.shortcoursesportal.com/disciplines/111/human-resource-management.html SHRM conferences, workshops, virtual events, and online programs: • Visit www.shrm.org/events to learn more about SHRM conferences and events. • Visit www.shrm.org/learningandcareer/learning/pages/seminars.aspx for more information about SHRM seminars. SHRM Learning System materials to prepare for the SHRM Certification exams, www.shrm.org/certification/learning/pages/default.aspx Programs offered by other HR associations/organizations: • HR People + Strategy (SHRM's Executive Network), www.hrps.org • Association for Talent Development (ATD), www.td.org • World at Work, The Total Rewards Association, www.worldatwork.org • International Society of Certified Employee Benefit Specialists (ISCEBS), www.iscebs.org
Self-driven activities (for example, books, articles, job shadowing, microlearning)	Research specific books and articles on individual functions from the SHRM bookstore (https://store.shrm.org/) or the websites for other organizations listed above. SHRM Toolkits on various topics, www.shrm.org/resourcesandtools/tools-and-samples/toolkits/pages/default.aspx Books: • *Developing Proficiency in HR: 7 Self-Directed Activities for HR Professionals,* Debra J. Cohen, Ph.D., SHRM, 2016. • *Fundamentals of Human Resource Management,* Raymond Noe, John Hollenbeck, Barry Gerhart, and Patrick Wright, McGraw-Hill, 2016. • *The Big Book of HR*, Barbara Mitchell and Cornelia Gamlem, Career Press, 2012. • *Looking to Hire an HR Leader? 14 Action Tools to Help You Decide, Find, and Keep the HR Professional Your Business Needs in a Competitive World,* Phyllis G. Hartman, SHRM, 2014. • *Never Get Lost Again: Navigating Your HR Career*, Nancy Glube and Phyllis Hartman, SHRM, 2009. • Take advantage of microlearning related to leadership using sources such as Degreed (www.degreed.com) or Pathgather (www.pathgather.com). SHRM resources: • Visit www.shrm.org/hr-today/trends-and-forecasting/special-reports-and-expert-views to read what thought leaders are saying about how to be successful in HR. • Visit community.shrm.org/home to network online with other professionals in HR using the SHRM Connect platform.
Professional/community activities (external involvement)	Join and participate in delivering programs, offering expertise, and networking with other HR professionals through SHRM and other organizations focused on specific HR functions: • Association for Talent Development (ATD), www.td.org • WorldatWork, The Total Rewards Association, www.worldatwork.org • International Society of Certified Employee Benefit Specialists (ISCEBS), www.iscebs.org Volunteer to assist nonprofit organizations with HR needs and problems to practice HR skills outside the workplace. • Get involved with local schools that offer HR programs, and teach or coach faculty, business advisory groups within the schools, or students about HR in the workplace. • Consider using crowd-sourced solutions for issues or HR professional networks like SHRM's Member2Member Solutions (www.shrm.org/resourcesandtools/tools-and-samples/member2member/pages/default.aspx), SHRM Connect, or LinkedIn groups.
Mentoring/coaching (self and others)	• Seek someone outside your HR areas of expertise to coach you on developing in other functions. • Mentor or coach someone new to HR.

CONTINUED ON NEXT PAGE

TABLE 8.1: GENERAL HR TECHNICAL COMPETENCY DEVELOPMENTAL ACTIVITIES CONTINUED

TYPE OF ACTIVITY	DETAILS
Assessments (focused on specific competency or subcompetency)	SHRM Competency Diagnostic Tools, www.shrm.org/LearningAndCareer/competency-model/pages/competency-diagnostic-tools.aspx
	The RBL Group assessments, www.rbl.net
	Seek certifications in general HR disciplines: • SHRM Certified Professional or SHRM Senior Certified Professional, www.shrm.org/certification • Professional in HR or Senior Professional in HR • Certified Compensation Professional • Certified Professional in Human Resources and Compensation • Certified Professional in Learning and Performance • Global Professional in Human Resource Management • Human Resource Business Professional • Human Resource Management Professional • Certified Employee Benefit Specialist • Compensation Management Specialist

PART IV:

Managing for Success

CHAPTER 9.

Helping Yourself— Competencies for Developing Others

This chapter explores specific management and leadership competencies you might need to develop your employees. Specifically noted from the SHRM Competency Model are these four:

TABLE 9.1: MANAGEMENT AND LEADERSHIP COMPETENCIES

Business Acumen	The knowledge, skills, abilities and other characteristics (KSAOs) needed to understand the organization's operations, functions, and external environment, and to apply business tools and analyses that inform HR initiatives and operations consistent with the overall strategic direction of the organization.
Consultation	The knowledge, skills, abilities and other characteristics (KSAOs) needed to work with organizational stakeholders in evaluating business challenges and identifying opportunities for the design, implementation, and evaluation of change initiatives, and to build ongoing support for HR solutions that meet the changing needs of customers and the business.
Critical Evaluation	The knowledge, skills, abilities and other characteristics (KSAOs) needed to collect and analyze qualitative and quantitative data, and to interpret and promote findings that evaluate HR initiatives and inform business decisions and recommendations.
Relationship Management	The knowledge, skills, abilities and other characteristics (KSAOs) needed to create and maintain a network of professional contacts within and outside of the organization, to build and maintain relationships, to work as an effective member of a team, and to manage conflict while supporting the organization.

Go back to the chapters that explore each of these competencies to get ideas and develop a plan for yourself. Consider assessing your own competencies; you can use the recommendations in Chapter 4 as well as those noted for each competency in Chapters 5-8.

Also worth considering is the Talent Management Subcompetency in the HR Technical Competency grouping. In addition, the following chart presents options for developing yourself in this area so that you can effectively develop others.

You can use Worksheet #3: Competency Development Planning Sheet to develop you own plan. You are highly encouraged to work on a selection of competencies, assessments, and plan development with your own manager, who can give you needed resources and support to develop yourself.

TABLE 9.2: TALENT MANAGEMENT/EMPLOYEE DEVELOPMENT COMPETENCY DEVELOPMENTAL ACTIVITIES

TYPE OF ACTIVITY	DETAILS
On the job	• Ask your reports how you can improve your delegation. Listen to their suggestions, and integrate them into your approach.
	• Coach someone on how to do something you are strong in but which he or she is not familiar.
	• Start a mentorship program within your organization.
	• Connect your employees with other role models and mentors who possess the skills they are trying to develop.
	• Delegate something you have not been comfortable delegating. Set it up to limit risk, and monitor the process as opposed to the results. Pay attention to your own feelings and reactions so you learn from the experience.
	• Ask your employees to lead meetings and report on information that they have researched or read about.
	• Hold regular team meetings to establish deliverables and priorities, and include discussion of successes and problems, obtaining input from all.
	• Identify someone who develops others effectively, and discuss your challenges in developing your reports; ask how he or she approaches talent management.
	• Maintain a development file on your team, including development needs, successful activities, and challenges, and look for patterns to see if your approach to development is the cause and if there are better ways to approach development.
	• Pay attention to employees' development successes, and recognize their accomplishments.
	• Development is a partnership activity. Arrange meetings with employees on development that focuses on their goals and desires, and plan developmental activities that serve your and their needs.
	• Individualize your approach, given that different employees need different development styles. Some employees need to be challenged, and others need to be gently lead or coached. Note the approach that is best for each.
	• Research learning approaches like gamification for employees who like to play online games.
	• Make sure you have available resources, money, and time for employees if you expect them to participate in developmental activities.
	• Schedule feedback sessions after assignments to discuss what happened and what was learned and how employees can use the learning going forward.
	• When an employee comes to you with a work problem, before giving a solution, ask how he or she might approach it.
	• Bring back learnings from conferences or meetings, and share them with your employees, discussing application to your workplace.
Group classes, workshops, conferences	College courses, certificates, and degrees in HR
	Programs offered by the Association for Talent Development (ATD), www.td.org
	SHRM conferences, workshops, virtual events, and online programs:
	• Visit www.shrm.org/events to learn more about SHRM conferences and events.
	• Visit www.shrm.org/learningandcareer/learning/pages/seminars.aspx for more information about SHRM seminars.

CONTINUED ON NEXT PAGE

TABLE 9.2: TALENT MANAGEMENT/EMPLOYEE DEVELOPMENT COMPETENCY DEVELOPMENTAL ACTIVITIES CONTINUED

TYPE OF ACTIVITY	DETAILS
Self-driven activities (for example, books, articles, job shadowing, microlearning)	Sign up for ATD newsletters and blogs, www.td.org/Publications/Newsletters. Books: • *Building the Learning Organization,* Michael J. Marquardt, ATD, 2011. • *So You Want to Start a Mentorship Program,* Nancy Kasmar, Knotted Road Press, 2014. • *Coaching Basics,* Lisa Haneberg, ATD, 2016. • *ASTD Competency Study: The Training & Development Profession Redefined,* William J. Rothwell, Justin Arneson, and Jennifer Naughton, ATD, 2013. • *Employee Development on a Shoestring,* Halelly Azulay, ASTD Press, 2013. • *Revolutionize Learning and Development,* Clark Quinn, Ph.D., Wiley, 2014. • *The Fifth Discipline: The Art & Practice of the Learning Organization,* Peter M. Senge, Doubleday, 2006. • *Managing the Millennials: Discover the Core Competencies for Managing Today's Workforce,* Chip Espinoza and Mick Ukleja, Wiley, 2016. • *Leadership Training* (ATD Workshop Series), Lou Russell, ATD, 2015. Look for programs offered by vendors like this one from LinkedIn: www.linkedin.com/learning/organizational-learning-and-development. SHRM Developing Employees toolkit, www.shrm.org/resourcesandtools/tools-and-samples/toolkits/pages/developingemployees.aspx. Manpower Report: *Millennial Careers: 2020 Vision,* www.manpowergroup.com/wps/wcm/connect/660ebf65-144c-489e-975c-9f838294c237/MillennialsPaper1_2020Vision_lo.pdf?MOD=AJPERES. "How to Make Microlearning Matter," Annie Murphy Paul, *HR Magazine,* May 2016, www.shrm.org/hr-today/news/hr-magazine/0516/pages/0516-microlearning.aspx. SHRM Resources: • Visit www.shrm.org/hr-today/trends-and-forecasting/special-reports-and-expert-views to read what thought leaders are saying about how to be successful in HR. • Visit community.shrm.org/home to network online with other professionals in HR using the SHRM Connect platform.
Professional/ community activities (external involvement)	Join and participate in delivering programs, offering expertise, and networking with other HR professionals through SHRM and other organizations focused on talent development, like the Association for Talent Development (ATD), www.td.org Volunteer to assist nonprofit organizations with training or employee development to practice skills outside the workplace. Get involved with local schools that offer HR programs, and teach or coach faculty, business advisory groups within the schools, or students about HR in the workplace.
Mentoring/ coaching (self and others)	Seek someone outside your HR areas of expertise to coach you on talent management and development.
Assessments (focused on specific competency or subcompetency)	SHRM Competency Diagnostic Tools, www.shrm.org/LearningAndCareer/competency-model/pages/competency-diagnostic-tools.aspx Study for and seek certification as a Certified Professional in Learning and Performance (CPLP), www.td.org/Certification.

CHAPTER 10.

Different Career Levels and Planning for Promotion

As defined by the SHRM Competency Model, all of the competencies essentially apply to all HR professionals in all positions. That said, some positions may require a higher level in a particular competency. For example, Relationship Management at a high level is critical for an individual who is in an employee relations position. There may be times when a position requires a lower level of a competency, like an early level HR payroll administrator who doesn't need a high level of Leadership and Navigation.

Another area of difference is based on various career stages. Early in an HR career, an individual may need to focus more heavily on the knowledge area of a competency versus on the ability or even the skill aspects.

With these differences in mind, the approach to development of competencies for each career stage needs to be modified for the individual. When planning developmental activities, consider the learning style, personal interests, and goals of each employee.

Likewise, consider the career level of the individual. SHRM recognizes four levels in much of its literature: early, mid-career, senior career, and executive.

All levels benefit from mentoring and coaching to develop competencies, given that even individuals at the senior or executive levels can be coached or mentored by someone who has more expertise either inside or outside the organization. An early level HR professional might be mentored or coached by his or her manager while an executive level professional might use a professional independent coach or mentor from outside the organization.

Early Career Level

Individuals at the early career level have little or no experience and often support HR functions versus leading them. They may at times lead small projects, but they are usually at a transactional level.

Developmental activities for this level might include shadowing a colleague who is at a higher career level or who is particularly proficient in a competency. With limited knowledge or experience, early career professionals are more likely to take an observer role as opposed to one that would include participating by offering suggestions.

Since someone at this level may still need knowledge, attending in-person courses at either colleges or universities or other professional programs would be beneficial. Online courses may be popular particularly if HR professionals are comfortable with this type of learning. You may want to recommend courses involving interaction between participants or to plan follow-up meetings to discuss the learning and how it applies to the workplace.

Attending conferences and learning how to network with colleagues outside the organization can be helpful at any level, but it is particularly important at the early career level.

Finally, reading daily or weekly news feeds focused on business and participating in practice exercises will help early level professionals grow and prepare to perform higher-level tasks.

Mid-Career Level

Mid-career professionals have some moderate level of experience. They may manage small to midsize projects and often lead or support operational functions. Competencies may be fairly well developed, but there may be gaps or the need for a focus on leadership competencies.

Shadowing colleagues can still be helpful at this level, but there would likely be more participation and discussion versus just observation because the mid-career individuals have more knowledge and experience.

Additional educational experiences through college courses or conferences may be appropriate for this group too, as would networking and membership in professional organizations.

At this level individuals have more to contribute and would likely benefit from project-based work, participation in planning activities, or a development assignment in another function.

Senior Career Level

At the senior level, HR professionals have significant experience. They typically fulfill a more operational, strategic, or consulting leadership role. These individuals often oversee large projects or programs or multiple functions. With significant experience and knowledge, they are able to translate strategies to plans. Competency development at this level usually focuses on higher-level leadership.

Participation in cross-functional teams and internal initiatives allows senior professionals to further develop competencies while contributing to the management of the organization, thus preparing for executive levels in the future.

Activities outside the organization, in communities of practice and even outside the home country, allow the senior professional to further grow.

Executive Career Level

At the executive career level, HR professionals have executive leadership experience and are the top HR consultant in their organization. They lead development of HR strategy and often participate in development of the organizational strategy. Peers for this level are the other executive managers in the organization. Competencies are usually highly developed, but individuals need to continue their professional growth to stay viable as leaders as conditions within the organization or industry change. In addition, HR leaders may be appropriate candidates for a CEO or other leadership role as they further hone their competencies.

Developmental activities at this level include networking internally with other executives and working on cross-functional teams related to organization initiatives. In addition, involvement in outside groups, professional organizations, and communities of practice is appropriate. Participation as a member of a committee, round table, or board with other professionals inside and outside HR circles provides networking and developmental opportunities.[1]

Final Thoughts

The four levels of HR professionals described here are not meant to limit developmental activities. As stated before, every person is unique in terms of competency level, and each organization is unique, so when choosing developmental activities for you or your HR reports, always keep your business mission, the desires and needs of the individual, and the availability of resources in mind.

Also, developing competencies in your HR people is critical if you want success in business. Not all employees will want to be the CEO someday, but if you help them see the value of growing and learning, you and they will be ready for future challenges.

Quick Reference Guide and Worksheets

Quick Reference Guide

The steps outlined here are merely suggestions for how you might proceed. As discussed before, you may have a clear understanding of HR competencies and what you need to develop in your reports. If that is the case, skip to Step 3 and begin to create your plan. If you have an interest in only one competency, go directly to that chapter to explore ideas for activities.

Step 1: Develop an understanding of HR competencies.
Read:
- Part I: The Business Case for Competencies
- Chapter 1. Challenges Facing HR Departments
- Chapter 2. Essential HR Competencies

Step 2: Connect HR competencies to your business needs, and determine gaps.
Read and apply:
- Part II: Linking HR Competencies to Business Outcomes
- Chapter 3. Aligning HR Functions with Competencies
- Chapter 4. Assessing Proficiencies

Step 3: Create a development plan.
Read and apply:
- Part III: Working through the Competencies with Developmental Activities
- Create a development plan that includes activities and goals:
  » Chapter 5. Interpersonal Competencies
  » Chapter 6. Business Competencies
  » Chapter 7. Leadership Competencies
  » Chapter 8. HR Technical Competencies

Step 4: Implement the plan.

Step 5:   Assess progress.
- Review Chapter 4 for assessment ideas, and then revisit Step 3 to modify the plan or create a new plan going forward.

Additional Help
- Chapter 9. Helping Yourself—Competencies for Developing Others. Create and implement a development plan for your own talent management competencies.
- Chapter 10. Career Levels and Planning for Promotion. Contains information on various career levels and competency development.

Appendix A: Worksheets
Worksheet #1: HR Competencies Needed for Your HR Function
Worksheet #2: Assessment Plan for Determining Competency Levels
Worksheet #3: Competency Development Planning Sheet

Worksheet #1: HR Competencies Needed for Your HR Functions

Organization's Key Competencies	If your organization has identified key competencies related to business goals, record them here.

Department/group/team Key Competencies	If your department, group or team has identified key competencies related to business goals, record them here.

SHRM HR Competencies	Identify the competencies below that are needed for your HR employees. This will likely be a combination of the organization and group competencies listed above. After you identify needed competencies rate the current level you think you have in your department/group/team. This may change after you do individual assessments for employees. Also, choose whether each is Core, Priority or Desired so you can focus on the most important first.

	We need (choose core, priority, desired by circling)	We are strong	We are weak
Communication	core, priority, desired		
Global and Cultural Effectiveness	core, priority, desired		
Relationship Management	core, priority, desired		
Business Acumen	core, priority, desired		
Consultation	core, priority, desired		
Critical Evaluation	core, priority, desired		
Ethical Practice	core, priority, desired		
Leadership and Navigation	core, priority, desired		
HR Expertise—includes the traditional HR functional areas	core, priority, desired		
Other notes/comments			

Worksheet# 2: Assessment Plan for Determining Competency Levels

Individual HR Competency Assessment Plan

Employee Name	Manager	Date

Competencies needed for current or future positions—list the core HR competencies you identified in Worksheet 1 that apply to this employee. After determining the approaches you will use, indicate which relate to which competency.

Competency	Method

Assessment methods for determining competency level of this employee.

Method	Target date	Notes/details
A-Employee meeting (can use interview questions in Chapter 4)		
B-Observations (O-T-J or specific assignments)		
C-Meet with co-workers, supervisors, customers/clients		
D-Past performance documents		
E-Learning management system information		
F-Career history		
G-Certifications (determine relation to HR competencies)		
H-Specific assessment tools (SHRM 180-360-Dept; others)		

Worksheet #3: Competency Development Planning Sheet

Name	Title	Date

Competency development involves a cooperative partnership between the employee, the manager and the organization. It includes plans for development in the current role and for future roles in the organization.

Strengths—competencies that have been identified as core/important for the current role or for future roles that where identified through assessment as strong in the individual.

1. _____

2. _____

3. _____

4. _____

5. _____

Development Needs—competencies that have been identified as core/important for the current role or for future roles that where identified through assessment as weak or non-existent in the individual.

1. _____

2. _____

3. _____

4. _____

5. _____

Development Focus—the areas chosen for this plan from above (may include both strengths that need further development or development needs).

1. _____

2. _____

3. _____

CONTINUED ON NEXT PAGE

Worksheet #3: Competency Development Planning Sheet Continued

Development Plan—activities, details and goals/deadlines for the individual. The employee and manager should meet on a regular/pre-set basis to discuss progress and completion. More than one approach should be used as appropriate for the particular competency, employee preference and learning style as well as available financial and time resources available.

Activity	Details	Timeframe/deadline
On the job		
Group classes, workshops, conferences		
Self-driven activities (books, articles, job shadowing, micro-learning, etc.)		
Professional/ community activities (external involvement)		
Mentoring/ coaching (self & others)		
Assessments (focused on specific competency or sub competency)		

Agreement—signed by employee and supervisor/manager to indicate agreement/commitment.

Employee	Manager	Date

APPENDIX B.

Spotlights: Real-Life Examples and Thoughts

Real-Life Examples and Thoughts

In preparation for this book, the author reached out to a group of executive level, experienced HR managers asking for their thoughts on developing their HR reports. The author is grateful for their ideas and expertise. The following individuals contributed thoughts, and some are specifically noted in this Appendix: Tim A. Baker, Karen Bolden, Columbus Brooks, Frank Cania, Fernán Cepero, Mary Cheddie, Brayton Connard, Robert Howard, Mary Lee Lison, Steve Miranda, Susan Renda, Ralph Ross, Phil Sukenik, David Twitchell, Hope Vaccaro, Sally Wade, Beverly Widger, and Mick Witenski.

People Don't Read

Most of the HR managers interviewed for this book agreed that reading is important for development of competencies, but most people don't read a lot today. Less available time, more available information in smaller bites through technology, or a hesitance to use one's own time on work "assignments" were all suggested as the reasons for reading less.

That said, those interviewed offered several suggestions for encouraging reports to read for development purposes. One manager succeeded at inspiring the HR staff to read by setting up an HR lunchtime book group. Assigning a book or article at first and then asking others to pick items and lead discussion resulted in not only better communication and critical thinking but also improved leadership competencies. Engagement was increased as staff shared ownership in selecting readings.

One company's CEO sometimes asks the total organization to read something related to the business and then discuss it within departments. He follows up by discussing the topic with his own reports and asks them for the feedback they gathered from their reports.

Internal Sharing and a Coordinated Approach

Fernán R. Cepero, MA, MS, PHR, SHRM-SCP, chief human resources officer (CHRO) and chief diversity officer of the YMCA of Greater Rochester in New York, says that one way his organization develops competencies is by recognizing the value of "internal sharing." Cross-functional development and teams are supported and encouraged. This helps HR staff develop both corporate understanding and communication and consultation competency.

Since competency development requires having experiences, the YMCA's approach to development organization wide is a 70/20/10 Learning Model:

- **Seventy percent of learning and development takes place from real-life, challenging on-the-job experiences, tasks, and problem solving.** This is the most important aspect of any learning and development plan. If you really want to grow, you'll have to stretch in uncomfortable areas; areas that may go against your natural strengths. For example, whether you gravitate toward team building or not, you can learn the behaviors of excellent team builders. You might even come to enjoy it. It's important not to confuse what you like to do with what's necessary to do.
- **Twenty percent of learning and development comes from coaching, feedback, and observing and working with role models.** Little happens without feedback tied to a goal. Find a coach; get a developmental partner; ask your supervisor for feedback on a regular basis; poll people you work with about what you should keep doing, keep doing with slight modifications, stop doing, and start doing.
- **Ten percent of learning and development comes from formal training.** Formal training can be delivered in a variety of ways including the Y-USA training system, your local YMCA, a third-party vendor, a college or university, online programs, self-study, and books.

For example, if you want to improve your performance related to the Philanthropy competency, you can create a development plan using the 70/20/10 Learning Model. You might first decide to attend a workshop sponsored by NAYDO (North American YMCA Development Organization) (10 percent). You might then find a coach who can help guide you along the way (20 percent), and you might apply your new knowledge and practice new skills while working on an annual campaign over several months (70 percent).[1]

Development Can Happen with Limited Time Resources

A senior vice president of a hospitality/food service company with 9,500 employees and 20 HR staff says that with a lean HR staff, development that directly relates to the needs of the organization is best. The company philosophy is to have cross-functional teams so HR can contribute perspective and learn about the work of the organization and other departments to better serve them. This approach helps HR employees develop since they are adding value and contributing while learning, even though they have limited time and serve a large population that is in many locations.

Assigning employees to work outside of their "normal" responsibilities to help the total team is another approach used in this company. One HR employee was preparing to lead training programs for hourly employees, and she didn't have a lot of experience working with that employee population. The VP assigned her to review and revise hourly recruiting forms, which needed updating, to help her get a better understanding of hourly positions and the people in that group.

Also, the company often moves managers around to develop them, and the VP has seen this technique work well for employees even when an employee is not happy about his or her new manager. Employees often learn more about how to be, or not to be, a manager themselves.

Culture and Size Impact Development

Phil Sukenik, SPHR, SHRM-SCP, PC, vice president of Restaurant Operations (formerly VP of human resources) for Hoss's Steak and Sea House, Inc. in Duncansville, PA, says "Both the culture and the size of the HR staff impact how you develop people. In a company with 5 HR staff and 2,500 employees you are driven to having people wearing many hats where people venture into new territories that require different competencies. At our company there are a lot of 'learn as you go' opportunities to grow and develop through stretch assignments that serve a business's needs. In addition, participation in professional organizations gives the smaller staff a chance to take advantage of the experience and knowledge of outside HR peers and experts."

Looking Outside

Having an organizational commitment to development is important in terms of resources. Often not just time but needed experiences go beyond what you can provide inside the organization. Beverly Widger, SPHR, SHRM-SCP, senior VP human resources at Mascoma Savings Bank in Lebanon, NH, says her organization supports development, and HR has a good budget to devote to it. By working with local universities, the organization is able to offer high-level programs that go beyond internal classes and programs.

Sally Wade, SHRM-SCP, SPHR, retired VP of HR for Mitsubishi Electric Power Products in Warrendale, PA, and president, AKCW Associates LLC, agrees that looking outward is necessary. "I believe it is important to encourage HR employees to learn about what other companies are doing in addition to formal knowledge transfer since there are so many ways to approach any situation in HR." Networking and professional memberships can support this approach.

Tap Employees for Development Ideas

HR managers use a variety of approaches to defining the competencies important to develop for their teams. Frank Cania, MSEmpL, SPHR, SHRM-SCP, president of driven HR-A USA Payroll Company in Pittsford, NY, relies on his team of HR professionals to help him choose the competencies on which to focus. The team members regularly project the future expectations of their clients. They are able to take full advantage of the synergies on the team to identify missing or weak areas and make plans for development. "I'm proud of how often one employee will identify an opportunity that may support the development goals of another and share that information with their peer."

Budget Limits Don't Have to Stop Development

Brayton Connard, SPHR, human resources director at Monroe County, Pittsford, NY, takes advantage of less costly opportunities to develop his team. "We have a very limited budget for development opportunities, so we try to leverage free resources, such as local seminars hosted by law firms (attorney advertising). We strongly prefer internal promotion, so we mentor and coach employees so that they learn our business and can be viable candidates for future promotional opportunities. One summer we did a series of lunch and learns where staff members with specialized knowledge took turns presenting to office colleagues. There is a statewide professional association that specializes in our industry. Because they are the only provider of industry training, we concentrate our limited training budget on sending as many staff members to the annual conference as possible."

He acknowledged that lean staffing means that he doesn't have many internal subject matter experts to choose from when selecting a coach or mentor, but due to a good retention rate driven by strong retirement benefits, he has time on his side. He can often predict when positions might come open, so he has time to "try out" different individuals in needed areas.

Certification Can Drive Development

Connard also cited his own development initiative as being driven by his need to maintain his HR certification. Knowing that he needs to take courses and attend programs or work on new projects for his certification renewal helps justify spending time and resources. The benefit is he continues to grow as a professional.

Networking Critical to Development

Columbus Brooks, founder of CBrooks HR Consulting, LLC in Pittsburgh, PA, has sometimes found reports less than willing to use networking as a way to develop since it may mean meetings and events beyond the regular workday. He has found from personal experience that networking with HR and other business colleagues is a beneficial development tool. "When I started my HR career my more experienced colleagues and mentors helped me learn about how to apply the HR knowledge I got in graduate school. In addition, I developed my Consultation and Communication competencies through the networking.

As I have gotten opportunities to manage other HR professionals and move up myself I try to help them understand how to network and get involved. Sometimes they need coaching on how to network. Once they see the value and start to get results they are more motivated. I follow up, ask them about their activities and show an interest to help them see that I value and support the extra effort."

One Size Does Not Fit All

Tim A. Baker, SHRM-SCP, SPHR, senior director for talent management and organizational development at Williamsburg-James City County Public Schools, says his experience working in three very different school districts as well as in the private sector has taught him that every employee and situation are different when it comes to development. In the large school district he worked in with 18,000 employees and 114 schools, the HR department had 60 employees. They came from HR, education, and even the private sector—making their development needs very diverse. However, he had a larger group to tap into to find coaches and mentors. By contrast, his current position includes only eight staff members in HR, and there are more limits to available internal help. Even the way the districts are funded in two different states drives the resources available for development. Each situation requires a different approach and strategy. He believes that managers need to be flexible and look for ideas, not just that one right answer or approach, to developing people.

Another thing that Baker pointed out is the need to develop people for succession even though they may leave to take another position before you have one ready for them. If not given a chance to grow, people may leave anyway or at least become frustrated in their current job. He even suggested that it may pay to alert an employee to an outside opportunity. If the person does leave, he or she is likely to have a greater respect for you and will be a good resource for you in the future.

HR Functional Areas and SHRM Competencies Chart

HR Expertise is structured into three higher-order knowledge domains: *People, Organization,* and *Workplace* (see figure below). These three domains of knowledge are further divided into 15 functional areas that describe with greater specificity the knowledge required to perform key HR activities, such as talent acquisition or engagement and retention.

Knowledge Domains and Functional Areas

Domain	Functional Area
People	HR Strategic Planning Talent Acquisition Employee Engagement & Retention Learning & Development Total Rewards
Organization	Structure of the HR Function Organizational Effectiveness & Development Workforce Management Employee & Labor Relations Technology Management
Workplace	HR in the Global Context Diversity & Inclusion Risk Management Corporate & Social Responsibility U.S. Employment Law & Regulations

SHRM Competency Model[1]

SHRM Body of Competency & Knowledge™

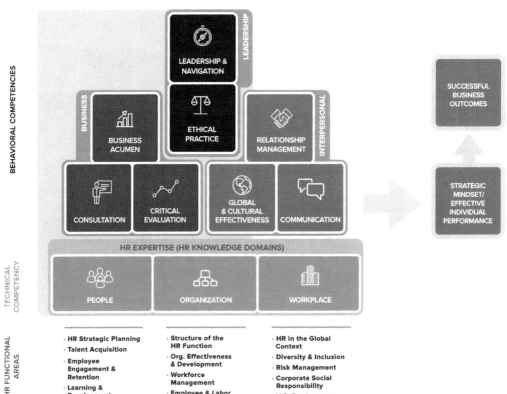

BEHAVIORAL COMPETENCIES

LEADERSHIP

BUSINESS

INTERPERSONAL

LEADERSHIP & NAVIGATION

ETHICAL PRACTICE

BUSINESS ACUMEN

RELATIONSHIP MANAGEMENT

CONSULTATION

CRITICAL EVALUATION

GLOBAL & CULTURAL EFFECTIVENESS

COMMUNICATION

HR EXPERTISE (HR KNOWLEDGE DOMAINS)

PEOPLE

ORGANIZATION

WORKPLACE

TECHNICAL COMPETENCY

SUCCESSFUL BUSINESS OUTCOMES

STRATEGIC MINDSET/ EFFECTIVE INDIVIDUAL PERFORMANCE

HR FUNCTIONAL AREAS

- HR Strategic Planning
- Talent Acquisition
- Employee Engagement & Retention
- Learning & Development
- Total Rewards

- Structure of the HR Function
- Org. Effectiveness & Development
- Workforce Management
- Employee & Labor Relations
- Technology Management

- HR in the Global Context
- Diversity & Inclusion
- Risk Management
- Corporate Social Responsibility
- U.S. Employment Law & Regulations*

*Applicable only to examinees testing within the U.S.

Proficiency Indicators from the SHRM BoCK for Different Levels of HR Staff[1]

Leadership & Navigation

Definition: *Leadership & Navigation* is defined as the knowledge, skills and abilities (KSAOs) needed to navigate the organization and accomplish HR goals, to create a compelling vision and mission for HR that aligns with the strategic direction and culture of the organization, to lead and promote organizational change, to manage the implementation and execution of HR initiatives, and to promote the role of HR as a key business partner.

Subcompetencies	Proficiency Indicators	
	For All HR Professionals	**For Advanced HR Professionals**
Navigating the organization—Works within the parameters of the organization's hierarchy, processes, systems and policies.	• Demonstrates an understanding of formal and informal work roles, leader goals and interests, and relationships among employees. • Facilitates communication and decision-making necessary to implement initiatives. • Uses an understanding of the organization's processes, systems and policies to facilitate the successful implementation of HR initiatives. • Uses awareness and understanding of the organization's political environment and culture to implement HR initiatives.	• Demonstrates an understanding of formal and informal work roles, leader goals and interests, and relationships among executives. • Uses an understanding of the complex relationships among the organization's formal and informal processes, systems and policies to facilitate the development and implementation of HR's strategic direction. • Uses an understanding of the organization's political environment to develop and implement HR's strategic direction, implement needed changes, and resolve talent needs and issues. • Uses an understanding of complex relationships among organizational leaders to facilitate the design, implementation and maintenance of initiatives proposed by other executives.
Vision—Defines and supports a coherent vision and long-term goals for HR that support the strategic direction of the organization.	• Embraces and supports the business unit's and/or organization's culture, values, mission and goals. • Defines actionable goals for the development and implementation of HR programs, practices and policies that support the strategic vision of HR and the organization. • Identifies opportunities to improve HR operations that better align with and support the strategic vision of HR and the organization. • Supports the implementation of HR programs, practices and policies that uphold the strategic vision of HR and the organization.	• Envisions the current and ideal future states of the HR function, organization and culture, to identify gaps and areas for improvement. • Develops the long-term strategic direction, vision and goals of HR and the organization, to close the gap between the current and ideal states of the HR function and the organization. • Develops a broad plan to achieve the strategic direction, vision and goals of HR and the organization. • Solicits feedback from executive-level stakeholders on strategic direction, vision and goals.

Leadership & Navigation continued

Subcompetencies	Proficiency Indicators	
	For All HR Professionals	**For Advanced HR Professionals**
Managing HR initiatives—Executes the implementation and management of HR projects or initiatives that support HR and organizational objectives.	• Defines and elaborates project requirements set forth by senior leadership. • Sets and monitors project goals and progress milestones. • Manages project budgets and resources. • Identifies and develops solutions for overcoming obstacles to the successful completion of projects. • Identifies and monitors the resources necessary to implement and maintain HR projects. • Identifies when resource allocation is inconsistent with project needs and makes adjustments as necessary. • Demonstrates agility and adaptability when project requirements, goals or constraints change.	• Translates HR's vision, strategic direction and long-term goals into specific projects and initiatives with clear timelines and goals. • Monitors the progress of HR initiatives toward achievement of HR's vision, strategic direction and long-term goals. • Collaborates with senior leadership to remove obstacles to the successful implementation of HR initiatives. • Obtains and deploys organizational resources and monitors their effectiveness. • Ensures accountability for the implementation of project plans and initiatives.
Influence—Inspires colleagues to understand and pursue the strategic vision and goals of HR and the organization.	• Builds credibility as an HR expert within and outside of the organization. • Promotes buy-in among organizational stakeholders for HR initiatives. • Motivates HR staff and other stakeholders to support HR's vision and goals. • Serves as an advocate for the organization or employees, when appropriate, to ensure advancement of the organization's strategic direction and goals.	• Promotes the role of the HR function in achieving the organization's mission, vision and goals. • Builds credibility for the organization regionally, nationally or internationally as an HR expert. • Serves as an influential voice for HR strategies, philosophies and initiatives within the organization. • Advocates for the implementation of evidence-based HR solutions. • Inspires HR staff, non-HR customers and executive-level organizational stakeholders to support and pursue the organization's strategic direction, vision and long-term goals. • Builds consensus among senior leaders about the organization's strategic direction and long-term goals.

Ethical Practice

Definition: *Ethical Practice* is defined as the knowledge, skills and abilities (KSAOs) needed to maintain high levels of personal and professional integrity, and to act as an ethical agent who promotes core values, integrity and accountability throughout the organization.

Subcompetencies	Proficiency Indicators	
	For All HR Professionals	For Advanced HR Professionals
Personal integrity— Demonstrates high levels of integrity in personal relationships and behaviors.	• Shows consistency between espoused and enacted values. • Acknowledges mistakes and demonstrates accountability for actions. • Recognizes personal biases and the biases of others, and takes steps to increase self-awareness. • Serves as a role model of personal integrity and high ethical standards.	• Brings potential conflicts of interest or unethical behaviors to the attention of senior leaders and other executives. • Helps others to identify and understand their biases.
Professional integrity— Demonstrates high levels of integrity in professional relationships and behaviors.	• Does not take adverse actions based on personal biases. • Maintains privacy, in compliance with laws and regulations mandating a duty to report unethical behavior. • Uses discretion appropriately when communicating sensitive information, and informs stakeholders of the limits of confidentiality and privacy. • Maintains current knowledge of ethics laws, standards, legislation and emerging trends that may affect organizational HR practice. • Leads HR investigations of employees in a thorough, timely and impartial manner. • Establishes oneself as credible and trustworthy. • Applies, and challenges when necessary, the organization's ethics and integrity policies. • Manages political and social pressures when making decisions and when implementing and enforcing HR programs, practices and policies. • Provides open, honest and constructive feedback to colleagues when situations involving questions of ethics arise.	• Withstands politically motivated pressure when developing or implementing strategy, initiatives or long-term goals. • Balances ethics, integrity, organizational success, employee advocacy and organizational mission and values when creating strategy, initiatives or long-term goals. • Establishes the HR team as a credible and trustworthy resource. • Promotes the alignment of HR and business practices with ethics laws and standards. • Makes difficult decisions that align with organizational values and ethics. • Applies power or authority appropriately.

Ethical Practice continued

Subcompetencies	Proficiency Indicators	
	For All HR Professionals	**For Advanced HR Professionals**
Ethical agent— Cultivates the organization's ethical environment, and ensures that policies and practices reflect ethical values.	• Empowers all employees to report unethical behaviors and conflicts of interest without fear of reprisal. • Takes steps to mitigate the influence of bias in HR and business decisions. • Maintains appropriate levels of transparency for HR programs, practices and policies. • Identifies, evaluates and communicates to leadership potential ethical risks and conflicts of interest. • Ensures that staff members have access to and understand the organization's ethical standards and policies.	• Advises senior management of organizational risks and conflicts of interest. • Collaborates with senior leaders to support internal ethics controls. • Develops and provides expertise for HR policies, standards, and other internal ethics controls (e.g., protection of employee confidentiality, standards for employee investigations) to minimize organizational risks from unethical practices. • Creates and oversees HR programs, practices and policies that drive an ethical culture, encourage employees to report unethical practices and behaviors, and protect the confidentiality of employees and data. • Communicates a vision for an organizational culture in which there is consistency between the organization's and employees' espoused and enacted values. • Develops HR programs, practices and policies that meet high standards of ethics and integrity. • Designs and oversees systems to ensure that all HR investigations are conducted in a thorough, timely and impartial manner. • Audits and monitors adherence to HR programs, practices and policies pertaining to ethics. • Designs and oversees learning and development programs covering ethics. • Implements and maintains a culture and organizational system that encourages all employees to report unethical practices and behaviors.

Relationship Management

Definition: *Relationship Management* is defined as the knowledge, skills and abilities (KSAOs) needed to create and maintain a network of professional contacts within and outside of the organization, to build and maintain relationships, to work as an effective member of a team, and to manage conflict while supporting the organization.

Subcompetencies	Proficiency Indicators	
	For All HR Professionals	**For Advanced HR Professionals**
Networking—Effectively builds a network of professional contacts both within and outside of the organization.	• Develops and maintains a network of professional contacts within the organization, including peers in both HR and non-HR roles, HR customers and stakeholders. • Develops and maintains a network of external partners (e.g., vendors). • Develops and maintains a network of professional colleagues in the HR community at large, for professional development and to fill business needs (e.g., identification of new talent).	• Creates opportunities for HR employees to network and build relationships with higher-level leaders in the organization and in the HR community at large. • Develops and maintains a network of contacts within the organization (e.g., senior leaders from other business units) and outside of the organization (e.g., members of legislative bodies, community leaders, union heads, external HR leaders).
Relationship building—Effectively builds and maintains relationships both within and outside of the organization.	• Develops and maintains mutual trust and respect with colleagues. • Develops and maintains a pattern of reciprocal exchanges of support, information and other valued resources with colleagues. • Demonstrates concern for the well-being of colleagues. • Establishes a strong and positive reputation, within and outside the organization, as an open and approachable HR professional. • Ensures that all stakeholder voices are heard and acknowledged. • Identifies and leverages areas of common interest among stakeholders, to foster the success of HR initiatives. • Develops working relationships with supervisors and HR leaders by promptly and effectively responding to work assignments, communicating goal progress and project needs, and managing work activities.	• Develops HR's objectives and goals for relationship management. • Develops and maintains relationships in the HR community at large through leadership positions in other organizations. • Leverages relationships to learn about best practices for and new approaches to building competitive advantage.

Relationship Management continued

Subcompetencies	Proficiency Indicators	
	For All HR Professionals	For Advanced HR Professionals
Teamwork—Participates as an effective team member, and builds, promotes and leads effective teams.	• Builds engaged relationships with team members through trust, task-related support and direct communication. • Fosters collaboration and open communication among stakeholders and team members. • Supports a team-oriented organizational culture. • Creates and/or participates in project teams comprised of HR and non-HR employees. • Embraces opportunities to lead a team. • Identifies and fills missing or unfulfilled team roles.	• Fosters an organizational culture that supports intra-organizational teamwork and collaboration (e.g., silo-busting). • Creates and leads teams with senior leaders from across the organization. • Designs and oversees HR initiatives that promote effective team processes and environments.
Conflict management—Manages and resolves conflicts by identifying areas of common interest among the parties in conflict.	• Resolves and/or mediates conflicts in a respectful, appropriate and impartial manner, and refers them to a higher level when warranted. • Identifies and addresses the underlying causes of conflict. • Facilitates difficult interactions among employees to achieve optimal outcomes. • Encourages productive and respectful task-related conflict, using it to facilitate change. • Serves as a positive role model for productive conflict. • Identifies and resolves conflict that is counterproductive or harmful.	• Designs and oversees conflict resolution strategies and processes throughout the organization. • Facilitates difficult interactions among senior leaders to achieve optimal outcomes. • Identifies and reduces potential sources of conflict when proposing new HR strategies or initiatives. • Mediates or resolves escalated conflicts.
Negotiation—Reaches mutually acceptable agreements with negotiating parties within and outside of the organization.	• Maintains a professional demeanor during negotiation discussions. • Applies an understanding of the needs, interests, issues and bargaining position of all parties to negotiation discussions. • Offers appropriate concessions to promote progress toward an agreement. • Adheres to applicable negotiation- and bargaining-related laws and regulations. • Evaluates progress toward an agreement. • Identifies an ideal solution or end state for negotiations, monitors progress toward that end state, and ends negotiations when appropriate.	• Negotiates with stakeholders within and outside of the organization in complex and high-stakes negotiations. • Defines the parameters of negotiating boundaries on behalf of the HR unit. • Achieves a mutually acceptable agreement in difficult and complex negotiations.

Communication

Definition: *Communication* is defined as the knowledge, skills and abilities (KSAOs) needed to effectively craft and deliver concise and informative communications, to listen to and address the concerns of others, and to transfer and translate information from one level or unit of the organization to another.

Subcompetencies	Proficiency Indicators	
	For All HR Professionals	**For Advanced HR Professionals**
Delivering messages— Develops and delivers, to a variety of audiences, communications that are clear, persuasive and appropriate to the topic and situation.	• Presents needed information to stakeholders and refrains from presenting unneeded information. • Uses an understanding of the audience to craft the content of communications (e.g., translates technical jargon), and chooses the best medium for communication. • Uses appropriate business terms and vocabulary. • Ensures that the delivered message is clear and understood by the listener. • Crafts clear, organized, effective and error-free messages. • Creates persuasive and compelling arguments.	• Demonstrates fluency in the business language of senior leaders. • Communicates difficult or negative messages in an honest, accurate, and respectful manner. • Comfortably presents to audiences of all sizes and backgrounds.
Exchanging organizational information— Effectively translates and communicates messages among organizational levels or units.	• Effectively communicates HR programs, practices and policies to both HR and non-HR employees. • Helps non-HR managers communicate HR issues. • Voices support for HR and organizational initiatives in communications with stakeholders. • Effectively communicates with senior HR leaders.	• Communicates HR's vision, strategy, goals and culture to senior leaders and HR staff. • Articulates to senior leaders the alignment of HR's strategies and goals with the organization's. • Implements policies and initiatives that create channels for open communication throughout the organization, across and within levels of responsibility. • Prepares and delivers to senior- and board-level audiences messages on important, high-visibility HR and organizational issues.

Communication continued

Subcompetencies	Proficiency Indicators	
	For All HR Professionals	For Advanced HR Professionals
Listening—Understands information provided by others.	• Listens actively and empathetically to others' views and concerns. • Welcomes the opportunity to hear competing points of view and does not take criticism personally. • Seeks further information to clarify ambiguity. • Promptly responds to and addresses stakeholder communications. • Interprets and understands the context of, motives for and reasoning in received communications. • Solicits feedback from senior leaders in other business units about the HR function.	• Develops an organizational culture in which upward communication is encouraged and senior leaders are receptive to staff views and opinions. • Establishes processes to gather feedback from the entire organization about the HR function.

Global & Cultural Effectiveness

Definition: *Global & Cultural Effectiveness* is defined as the knowledge, skills and abilities (KSAOs) needed to value and consider the perspectives and backgrounds of all parties, to interact with others in a global context, and to promote a diverse and inclusive workplace.

Subcompetencies	Proficiency Indicators	
	For All HR Professionals	**For Advanced HR Professionals**
Operating in a diverse workplace— Demonstrates openness and tolerance when working with people from different cultural traditions.	• Demonstrates a general awareness and understanding of and respect for cultural differences and issues. • Adapts behavior to navigate different cultural conditions, situations and people. • Demonstrates acceptance of colleagues from different cultures. • Promotes the benefits of a diverse and inclusive workforce. • Promotes inclusion in daily interactions with others. • Conducts business with an understanding of and respect for cross-cultural differences in customs and acceptable behaviors.	• Drives a culture that values diversity and inclusion. • Advocates for the strategic connection of diversity and inclusion practices to organizational success.
Operating in a global environment— Effectively manages globally influenced workplace requirements to achieve organizational goals.	• Demonstrates an understanding, from a global perspective, of the organization's line of business. • Tailors HR initiatives to local needs by applying an understanding of cultural differences. • Conducts business with an understanding of and respect for differences in rules, laws, regulations and accepted business operations and practices. • Applies knowledge of global trends when implementing or maintaining HR programs, practices and policies. • Operates with a global mindset while remaining sensitive to local issues and needs. • Manages contradictory or paradoxical practices, policies and cultural norms, to ensure harmony and success across a dispersed workforce.	• Creates an HR strategy that incorporates the organization's global competencies and perspectives on organizational success. • Uses expert knowledge about global HR trends, economic conditions, labor markets and legal environments to set HR's strategic direction and to inform development and implementation of HR initiatives. • Uses expert knowledge about global HR trends, economic conditions, labor markets and legal environments to evaluate the impact of diversity and inclusion on the organization's HR strategy.

Global & Cultural Effectiveness continued

Subcompetencies	Proficiency Indicators	
	For All HR Professionals	For Advanced HR Professionals
Advocating for a diverse and inclusive workplace— Designs, implements and promotes organizational policies and practices to ensure diversity and inclusion in the workplace.	• Supports an organizational culture that values diversity and promotes inclusion. • Uses the organization's policies and philosophy toward diversity and inclusion to inform business decisions and implementation of HR programs, practices and policies. • Designs, recommends, implements, and/or audits HR programs, practices and policies intended to ensure diversity and inclusion. • Ensures that HR programs, practices and policies are applied consistently and respectfully to all staff.	• Develops HR initiatives, programs and policies that support the organization's policies and philosophy toward diversity and inclusion. • Ensures that learning and development programs (or other appropriate interventions) about diversity and cultural sensitivity are provided to employees at all levels of the organization. • Develops HR initiatives that will be applied consistently and fairly to all staff. • Drives an HR strategy that leverages diversity, inclusion and cultural differences for organizational success.

Business Acumen

Definition: *Business Acumen* is defined as the knowledge, skills and abilities (KSAOs) needed to understand the organization's operations, functions and external environment, and to apply business tools and analyses that inform HR initiatives and operations consistent with the overall strategic direction of the organization.

Subcompetencies	Proficiency Indicators	
	For All HR Professionals	**For Advanced HR Professionals**
Business and competitive awareness— Understands the organization's operations, functions, products and services, and the competitive, economic, social and political environments in which the organization operates.	• Uses organizational and external resources to learn about the organization's business operations, functions, products and services. • Uses organizational and external resources to learn about the political, economic, social, technological, legal and environmental (PESTLE) trends that influence the organization. • Applies knowledge of the organization's business operations, functions, products and services, in order to implement HR solutions and inform business decisions. • Applies knowledge of the organization's industry and PESTLE trends, in order to implement HR solutions and inform HR decisions.	• Gathers and applies business intelligence about PESTLE trends to define HR's strategic direction and long-term goals. • Applies expert knowledge of the organization's business operations, functions, products and services when setting HR's strategic direction and long-term goals. • Applies an understanding of the labor market when developing a strategy to manage and compete for talent. • Participates in advocacy activities involving government policy and proposed regulations related to the organization's HR strategies and long-term goals.
Business analysis— Applies business metrics, principles and technologies to inform and address business needs.	• Uses cost-benefit analysis, organizational metrics and key performance indicators to inform business decisions. • Applies principles of finance, marketing, economics, sales, technology, law and business systems to internal HR programs, practices and policies. • Uses HR information systems (HRIS) and business technology to solve problems and address needs.	• Designs, implements, and evaluates HR initiatives with consideration of value-added, ROI, utility, revenue, profit and loss statements and other business indicators. • Uses risk assessment to inform HR's and the organization's strategic direction and long-term goals. • Determines the budget and resource requirements of HR initiatives. • Develops HRIS and business technology to solve business problems and address needs. • Examines organizational problems and opportunities in terms of integrating HR solutions that maximize ROI and strategic effectiveness.

Business Acumen continued

Subcompetencies	Proficiency Indicators	
	For All HR Professionals	**For Advanced HR Professionals**
Strategic alignment— Aligns HR strategy, communications, initiatives and operations with the organization's strategic direction.	• Demonstrates an understanding of the relationship between effective HR and effective core business functions. • Aligns decisions with HR's and the organization's strategic direction and goals. • Makes the business case, or provides the data to build the case, for HR initiatives and their influence on efficient and effective organizational functioning (e.g., ROI for HR initiatives).	• Defines and communicates HR's and the organization's strategy, goals and challenges in terms of business results. • Aligns HR's strategic direction and long-term goals with the organization's overall business strategy and objectives. • Applies the perspective of systems thinking to make HR and business decisions. • Drives key business results by developing strategies and long-term goals that account for senior leaders' input. • Serves as a strategic contributor to organizational decision-making on fiscal issues, product/service lines, operations, human capital and technology. • Evaluates all proposed business cases for HR initiatives.

Consultation

Definition: *Consultation* is defined as the knowledge, skills and abilities (KSAOs) needed to work with organizational stakeholders in evaluating business challenges and identifying opportunities for the design, implementation and evaluation of change initiatives, and to build ongoing support for HR solutions that meet the changing needs of customers and the business.

Subcompetencies	Proficiency Indicators	
	For All HR Professionals	**For Advanced HR Professionals**
Evaluating business challenges—Works with business partners and leaders to identify business challenges and opportunities for HR solutions.	• Develops an understanding of the organization's current and future HR challenges, and helps to identify HR needs and opportunities for improvement. • Identifies current and future HR-related threats and liabilities. • Identifies existing HR programs, practices and policies that impede or support business success.	• Works with senior leadership to identify how HR can improve business outcomes and support the organization's strategic direction and long-term goals.
Designing HR solutions—Works with business partners and leaders to design HR solutions and initiatives that meet business needs.	• Offers, in partnership with stakeholders, HR solutions for business needs that are creative, innovative, effective and based on best practices and/or research. • Provides guidance to non-HR managers regarding HR practices, compliance, laws, regulations and ethics. • Defines clear goals and outcomes for HR solutions, using them to drive solution design.	• Works with key internal customers to identify initiatives that minimize threats and liabilities. • Determines the strategic approach to remediation of HR-related threats and liabilities. • Works with business leaders to create innovative, evidence-based talent management strategies that align with and drive the organization's strategy. • Designs and oversees evidence-based long-term strategic HR and business solutions.
Implementing and supporting HR solutions—Works with business partners and leaders to implement and support HR solutions and initiatives.	• Provides guidance to non-HR managers and business unit teams on implementation of HR-related solutions. • Works with business partners to overcome obstacles to implementation of HR solutions. • Provides follow-up to and ongoing support for implementation of HR solutions, to ensure their continued effectiveness. • Ensures that implementation of HR solutions adheres to defined goals and outcomes.	• Provides ongoing support and HR solutions to business unit leaders on the organization's strategic direction. • Encourages staff and other leaders to provide input on strategic HR and business decisions. • Works with senior leaders to overcome strategic obstacles to implementation of HR initiatives. • Integrates HR solutions with related organizational processes, systems and other business or management initiatives.

Consultation continued

Subcompetencies	Proficiency Indicators	
	For All HR Professionals	For Advanced HR Professionals
Change management—Leads and supports maintenance of or changes in strategy, organization and/or operations.	• Recommends ways to improve HR programs, practices and policies. • Promotes buy-in among organizational stakeholders when implementing change initiatives. • Builds buy-in among staff for organizational change. • Aligns and deploys HR programs to support change initiatives.	• Works with other senior executives to identify when and where change is or is not needed. • Builds buy-in among senior leadership and staff at all levels for organizational change. • Defines change objectives and goals. • Oversees implementation of change initiatives across business units and throughout the organization. • Partners with other business leaders to achieve change objectives and goals. • Provides support to HR staff at all levels during change initiatives.
Customer interaction—Provides high-quality customer service and contributes to a strong customer service culture.	• Identifies, defines and clarifies customer needs and requirements, and reports on the status of HR services provided and results achieved. • Responds promptly, courteously and openly to customer requests, and takes ownership of customer needs. • Identifies and resolves risks and early-stage problems in meeting customer needs. • Manages interactions with vendors and suppliers to maintain service quality.	• Designs and oversees HR programs, practices and policies that ensure a strong, high-quality customer service culture in the HR function. • Oversees HR's customer service objectives and outcomes. • Identifies larger system needs and issues influencing market requirements, and engages outside stakeholders to help meet requirements that go beyond HR's functional assignment. • Develops and promotes an organizational culture that excels at meeting customer needs.

Critical Evaluation

Definition: *Critical Evaluation* is defined as the knowledge, skills and abilities (KSAOs) needed to collect and analyze qualitative and quantitative data, and to interpret and promote findings that evaluate HR initiatives and inform business decisions and recommendations.

Subcompetencies	Proficiency Indicators	
	For All HR Professionals	**For Advanced HR Professionals**
Data advocate—Understands and promotes the importance and utility of data.	• Demonstrates an understanding of the importance of using data to inform business decisions and recommendations. • Promotes the importance of evidence-based decision-making. • Promotes the importance of validating HR programs, practices and policies to ensure that they achieve desired outcomes. • Identifies decision points that can be informed by data and evidence.	• Promotes the role of evidence in setting and validating HR's strategic direction and long-term goals. • Supports an organizational culture that promotes the collection and incorporation of data (e.g., risks, economic and environmental factors) into decision-making, and supports the organizational processes, policies and procedures to do so. • Promotes the utility of HR metrics for understanding organizational performance. • Ensures that the HR function uses data to inform decision-making and the development and evaluation of HR initiatives.
Data gathering—understands how to determine data utility, and identifies and gathers data to inform organizational decisions.	• Maintains working knowledge of data collection, research methods, benchmarks and HR metrics. • Identifies sources of the most relevant data for solving organizational problems and answering questions. • Gathers data using appropriate methods (e.g., surveys, focus groups) to inform and monitor organizational solutions. • Scans external sources for data relevant to the organization (e.g., risks, economic and environmental factors). • Benchmarks HR initiatives and outcomes against the organization's competition and other relevant comparison groups.	• Ensures that resources and processes are in place to facilitate systematic collection of data, to inform HR's strategic direction and long-term goals. • Identifies new sources of data or new methods of data collection to inform and evaluate HR initiatives. • Interacts with senior leaders outside the organization to collect data relevant to HR.

Critical Evaluation continued

Subcompetencies	Proficiency Indicators	
	For All HR Professionals	For Advanced HR Professionals
Data analysis—Analyzes data to evaluate HR initiatives and business challenges.	• Maintains working knowledge of statistics and measurement concepts. • Identifies potentially misleading or flawed data. • Conducts analyses to identify evidence-based best practices, evaluate HR initiatives and determine critical findings. • Maintains objectivity when interpreting data.	• Maintains advanced knowledge of statistics and measurement concepts. • Oversees comprehensive and systematic evaluations of the organization's HR programs, practices and policies. • Critically reviews and interprets the results of analyses to identify evidence-based best practices, evaluate HR initiatives and determine critical findings.
Evidence-based decision-making—Uses the results of data analysis to inform the best course of action.	• Reports key findings to senior business and HR leaders. • Uses research findings to evaluate different courses of action and their impacts on the organization. • Applies data-driven knowledge and best practices from one situation to the next, as appropriate. • Ensures that HR programs, practices and policies reflect research findings and best practices. • Objectively examines HR programs, practices and policies in light of data.	• Communicates to other senior leaders in the organization critical data analysis findings and their implications for HR's strategic direction and goals. • Uses research findings to inform HR's strategic direction and long-term goals. • Develops best practices based on evidence from industry literature, peer-reviewed research and other sources, including experience. • Sponsors evidence-based initiatives for process improvement.

Functional Area #1: HR Strategic Planning

Definition: *HR Strategic Planning* involves the activities necessary for developing, implementing and managing the strategic direction required to achieve organizational success and to create value for stakeholders.

Proficiency Indicators	
For All HR Professionals	**For Advanced HR Professionals**
• Uses the perspective of systems thinking to understand how the organization operates. • Informs business decisions with knowledge of the strategy and goals of HR and the organization. • Develops and implements an individual action plan for executing HR's strategy and goals. • Uses benchmarks, industry metrics and workforce trends to understand the organization's market position and competitive advantage. • Informs HR leadership of new or overlooked opportunities to align HR's strategy with the organization's. • Provides HR leadership with timely and accurate information required for strategic decision-making.	• Identifies the ways in which the HR function can support the organization's strategy and goals. • Engages other business leaders in strategic analysis and planning. • Evaluates HR's critical activities in terms of value added, impact and utility, using cost-benefit analysis, revenue, profit-and-loss estimates and other leading or lagging indicators. • Provides HR-focused expertise to other business leaders when formulating the organization's strategy and goals. • Develops and implements HR strategy, vision and goals that align with and support the organization's strategy and goals. • Ensures that HR strategy creates and sustains the organization's competitive advantage.

Functional Area #2: Talent Acquisition

Definition: *Talent Acquisition* encompasses the activities involved in building and maintaining a workforce that meets the needs of the organization.

Proficiency Indicators	
For All HR Professionals	**For Advanced HR Professionals**
• Understands the talent needs of the organization or business unit. • Uses a wide variety of talent sources and recruiting methods to attract qualified applicants. • Uses technology (e.g., social media, applicant tracking software [ATS]) to support effective and efficient approaches to sourcing and recruiting employees. • Promotes and uses the employer value proposition and employment brand for sourcing and recruiting applicants. • Uses the most appropriate hiring methods to best evaluate a candidate's technical skills, organizational fit and alignment with the organization's competency needs. • Conducts appropriate pre-employment screening. • Implements effective onboarding and orientation programs for new employees. • Designs job descriptions to meet the organization's resource needs.	• Analyzes staffing levels and projections, to forecast workforce needs. • Develops strategies for sourcing and acquiring a workforce that meets the organization's needs. • Establishes an employer value proposition and employment brand that supports recruitment of high-quality job applicants. • Designs and oversees effective strategies for sourcing, recruiting and evaluating qualified job candidates. • Designs and oversees employee onboarding and assimilation processes. • Designs and oversees valid and systematic programs for assessing the effectiveness of talent acquisition activities that meet the organization's needs.

Functional Area #3: Employee Engagement & Retention

Definition: *Employee Engagement & Retention* refers to activities aimed at retaining high-performing talent, solidifying and improving the relationship between employees and the organization, creating a thriving and energized workforce, and developing effective strategies to address appropriate performance expectations from employees at all levels.

Proficiency Indicators	
For All HR Professionals	**For Advanced HR Professionals**
• Designs, administers, analyzes and interprets surveys of employee attitudes (e.g., engagement, job satisfaction) and culture. • Administers and supports HR and organizational programs designed to improve employee attitudes and culture (e.g., social events, telecommuting policies, recognition, job enlargement/enrichment, workplace flexibility). • Identifies program opportunities to create more engaging or motivating jobs (e.g., job enrichment/enlargement). • Monitors changes in turnover and retention metrics, and ensures that leadership is aware of such changes. • Coaches supervisors on creating positive working relationships with their employees. • Trains stakeholders on use of organization's performance management systems (e.g., how to enter performance goals, make ratings). • Helps stakeholders understand the elements of satisfactory employee performance and performance management. • Implements and monitors processes that measure effectiveness of performance management systems.	• In collaboration with other leaders, defines an organizational strategy to create an engaged workforce. • Implements best practices for employee retention in HR programs, practices and policies (e.g., realistic job previews [RJP], career development programs, employee socialization). • Communicates to other senior leaders the results of surveys of employee attitudes and culture. • Designs and oversees an action plan to address the findings of employee attitude surveys. • Designs and oversees HR and organizational programs designed to improve employee attitudes (e.g., social events, telecommuting policies, recognition, job enlargement/enrichment, workplace flexibility). • Holistically monitors the organization's metrics on employee attitudes, turnover and retention, and other information about employee engagement and retention. • Designs and oversees best practices-based employee performance management systems that meet the organization's talent management needs. • Designs and oversees processes to measure the effectiveness of performance management systems.

Functional Area #4: Learning & Development

Definition: *Learning & Development* activities enhance the knowledge, skills and abilities (KSAOs) and competencies of the workforce in order to meet the organization's business needs.

Proficiency Indicators	
For All HR Professionals	**For Advanced HR Professionals**
• Uses best practices to evaluate data on competency gaps. • Creates individual development plans (IDPs) in collaboration with supervisors and employees. • Uses best practices to develop and deliver learning and development activities that close gaps in employees' competencies and skills. • Uses all available resources (e.g., vendors) to develop and deliver effective learning and development programs. • Creates internal social networks to facilitate knowledge-sharing among employees. • Administers and supports programs to promote knowledge transfer.	• Designs and oversees efforts to collect data on competency gaps. • Provides guidance to identify and develop critical competencies that meet the organization's talent needs. • Monitors the effectiveness of programs for emerging leaders and leadership development. • Creates long-term organizational strategies to develop talent. • Creates strategies to ensure the retention of organizational knowledge.

Functional Area #5: Total Rewards

Definition: *Total Rewards* refers to the design and implementation of compensation systems and benefit packages, which employers use to attract and retain employees.

Proficiency Indicators	
For All HR Professionals	**For Advanced HR Professionals**
• Collects, compiles and interprets compensation and benefits data from various sources (e.g., remuneration surveys, labor market trends). • Implements appropriate pay, benefit, incentive, separation and severance systems and programs. • Complies with best practices for and laws and regulations governing compensation and benefits. • Differentiates between government-mandated, government-provided and voluntary benefit approaches. • Performs accurate job evaluations to determine appropriate compensation.	• Designs and oversees organizational compensation and benefits philosophies, strategies and plans that align with the organization's strategic direction and talent needs. • Designs and oversees executive compensation approaches that directly connect individual performance to organizational success. • Ensures the internal equity of compensation systems.

Functional Area #6: Structure of the HR Function

Definition: *Structure of the HR Function* encompasses the people, processes, theories and activities involved in the delivery of HR-related services that create and drive organizational effectiveness.

Proficiency Indicators	
For All HR Professionals	**For Advanced HR Professionals**
• Adapts work style to fit the organization's HR service model (e.g., centralized vs. decentralized), to ensure timely and consistent delivery of services to stakeholders. • Seeks feedback from stakeholders to identify opportunities for HR function improvements • Acts as HR point-of-service contact for key stakeholders within a division or group. • Provides consultation on HR issues to all levels of leadership and management. • Coordinates with other HR functions to ensure timely and consistent delivery of services to stakeholders. • Ensures that outsourced and/or automated HR functions are integrated with other HR activities. • Analyzes and interprets key performance indicators to understand the effectiveness of the HR function.	• Designs and implements the appropriate HR service model for the organization (e.g., centralized vs. decentralized), to ensure efficient and effective delivery of services to stakeholders. • Creates long-term goals that address feedback from stakeholders identifying opportunities for HR function improvements. • Ensures that all elements of the HR function (e.g., recruiting, talent management, compensation and benefits, learning and development) are aligned and integrated, and provide timely and consistent delivery of services to stakeholders. • Identifies opportunities to improve HR operations by outsourcing work or implementing technologies that automate HR functions (e.g., time, payroll). • Designs and oversees programs to collect, analyze and interpret key performance indicators (e.g., balanced scorecard) to evaluate the effectiveness of HR activities in supporting organizational success.

Functional Area #7: Organizational Effectiveness & Development

Definition: *Organizational Effectiveness & Development* concerns the overall structure and functionality of the organization, and involves measurement of long- and short-term effectiveness and growth of people and processes and implementation of necessary organizational change initiatives.

Proficiency Indicators	
For All HR Professionals	**For Advanced HR Professionals**
• Ensures that key documents and systems (e.g., job postings and descriptions, performance management systems) accurately reflect workforce activities. • Supports change initiatives to increase the effectiveness of HR systems and processes. • Identifies areas in the organization's structures, processes and procedures that need change. • Provides recommendations for eliminating barriers to organizational effectiveness and development. • Collects and analyzes data on the value of HR initiatives to the organization.	• Aligns HR's strategy and activities with the organization's mission, vision, values and strategy. • Regularly monitors results against performance standards and goals in support of the organization's strategy. • Establishes measurable goals and objectives to create a culture of accountability. • Consults on, plans and designs organizational structures that align with the effective delivery of activities in support of the organization's strategy. • Assesses organizational needs to identify critical competencies for operational effectiveness. • Designs and oversees change initiatives to increase the effectiveness of HR systems and processes. • Ensures that HR initiatives demonstrate measurable value to the organization.

Functional Area #8: Workforce Management

Definition: *Workforce Management* refers to HR practices and initiatives that allow the organization to meet its talent needs (e.g., workforce planning, succession planning) and to close critical competency gaps.

Proficiency Indicators	
For All HR Professionals	**For Advanced HR Professionals**
• Identifies gaps in workforce competencies and misalignment of staffing levels. • Implements approaches (e.g., buy or build) to ensure that appropriate workforce staffing levels and competencies exist to meet the organization's goals and objectives. • Plans short-term strategies to develop workforce competencies that support the organization's goals and objectives. • Administers and supports approaches (e.g., succession plans, high-potential development programs) to ensure that the organization's leadership needs are met. • Supports strategies for restructuring the organization's workforce (e.g., mergers and acquisitions, downsizing).	• Evaluates how the organization's strategy and goals align with future and current staffing levels and workforce competencies. • Develops strategies to maintain a robust workforce that has the talent to carry out the organization's current and future strategy and goals. • Coordinates with business leaders to create strategies (e.g., succession planning, leadership development, training) that address the organization's leadership needs. • Develops strategies for restructuring the organization's workforce (e.g., mergers and acquisitions, downsizing).

Functional Area #9: Employee & Labor Relations

Definition: *Employee & Labor Relations* refers to any dealings between the organization and its employees regarding the terms and conditions of employment.

Proficiency Indicators	
For All HR Professionals	**For Advanced HR Professionals**
• Supports interactions with union and other employee representatives. • Supports the organization's interests in union-management activities. • Assists and supports the organization in the collective bargaining process. • Participates in or facilitates alternative dispute resolution (ADR) processes (e.g., arbitration, mediation). • Makes recommendations for addressing other types of employee representation (e.g., governmental, legal). • Develops and implements workplace policies, handbooks and codes of conduct. • Provides guidance to employees on the terms and implications of their employment agreement and the organization's policies and procedures (e.g., employee handbook). • Consults managers on how to supervise difficult employees, handle disruptive behaviors and respond with the appropriate level of corrective action. • Conducts investigations into employee misconduct and suggests disciplinary action when necessary. • Manages employee grievance and discipline processes. • Resolves workplace labor disputes internally.	• Manages interactions and negotiations with union and other employee representatives (e.g., governmental, legal). • Serves as the primary representative of the organization's interests in union-management activities (e.g., negotiations, dispute resolution). • Manages the collective bargaining process. • Consults on and develops an effective organized labor strategy (e.g., avoidance, acceptance, adaptation) to achieve the organization's desired impact on itself and its workforce. • Educates employees, managers and leaders at all levels about the organization's labor strategy (e.g., avoidance, acceptance, adaptation) and its impact on the achievement of goals and objectives. • Educates employees at all levels about changes in the organization's policies. • Coaches and counsels managers on how to operate within the parameters of organizational policy, labor agreements and employment agreements. • Oversees employee investigations and discipline.

Functional Area #10: Technology Management

Definition: *Technology Management* involves the use of existing, new and emerging technologies to support the HR function, and the development and implementation of policies and procedures governing the use of technologies in the workplace.

Proficiency Indicators	
For All HR Professionals	**For Advanced HR Professionals**
• Implements and uses technology solutions that support or facilitate delivery of effective HR services and storage of critical employee data. • Implements HR information systems (HRIS) that integrate with and complement other enterprise information systems. • Develops and implements organizational standards and policies for maintaining confidentiality of employee data. • Uses technologies in a manner that protects workforce data. • Provides guidance to stakeholders on effective standards and policies for use of technologies in the workplace (e.g., social media, corporate and personal e-mail, internet messaging). • Coordinates and manages vendors implementing HR technology solutions. • Uses technologies that collect, access and analyze data and information, in order to understand business challenges and recommend evidence-based solutions.	• Evaluates and implements technology solutions that support the achievement of HR's strategic direction, vision and goals. • Evaluates and selects vendors to provide HR technology solutions. • Designs and implements technology systems that optimize and integrate HR functional areas. • Develops and implements technology-driven self-service approaches that enable managers and employees to perform basic people-related transactions (e.g., scheduling, timekeeping, compensation administration, benefit enrollment, information changes).

Functional Area #11: HR in the Global Context

Definition: *HR in the Global Context* focuses on the role of the HR professional in managing global workforces to achieve organizational objectives.

Proficiency Indicators	
For All HR Professionals	**For Advanced HR Professionals**
• Addresses global issues that influence day-to-day HR activities and makes recommendations for business solutions. • Maintains up-to-date knowledge of global political, economic, social, technological, legal and environmental (PESTLE) factors and their influence on the organization's workforce. • Administers and supports HR activities associated with a global workforce. • Implements and conducts audits of global HR practices. • Maintains knowledge of global HR trends and best practices. • Balances with local needs the organization's desire for standardization of HR programs, practices and policies. • Builds relationships with global stakeholders. • Manages the day-to-day activities associated with international (i.e., expatriate) assignments.	• Recognizes and responds to global issues that influence the organization's human capital strategy. • Consults with business leaders on global PESTLE factors and their influence on the organization's workforce. • Develops a comprehensive organizational strategy that addresses global workforce issues. • Consults with business leaders to define global competencies and embed them throughout the organization. • Identifies opportunities to achieve efficiencies and cost savings by moving work (e.g., offshoring, on-shoring, near-shoring). • Designs and oversees programs for international (i.e., expatriate) assignments that support the organization's human capital strategy.

Functional Area #12: Diversity & Inclusion

Definition: *Diversity & Inclusion* encompasses activities that create opportunities for the organization to leverage the unique backgrounds and characteristics of all employees to contribute to its success.

Proficiency Indicators	
For All HR Professionals	**For Advanced HR Professionals**
• Provides mentoring, training, guidance and coaching on cultural differences and practices to employees at all levels of the organization. • Consults with managers about distinctions between performance issues and cultural differences. • Develops and maintains knowledge of current trends and HR management best practices relating to diversity and inclusion (D&I). • Contributes to development and maintenance of an organizational culture that values a diverse and inclusive workforce (e.g., conducts diversity training). • Identifies opportunities to enhance the fairness of organizational policies and procedures to all employees (e.g., removes demographic barriers to success). • Identifies and implements workplace accommodations. • Demonstrates support to internal and external stakeholders for the organization's D&I efforts.	• Incorporates D&I goals into all HR programs, practices and policies. • Advocates for incorporation of diversity goals into the organization's strategic plan. • Develops, implements and oversees, in conjunction with other business leaders, enterprise-wide programs, practices and policies that lead to a diverse workforce. • Designs and oversees HR programs, practices and policies supporting the development and maintenance of an organizational culture that values and promotes a diverse and inclusive workforce. • Designs and oversees HR programs, practices and policies that encourage employees to take advantage of opportunities for working with those who possess diverse set of experiences and backgrounds. • Ensures that HR staff members have up-to-date knowledge of current trends and HR management best practices relating to D&I.

Functional Area #13: Risk Management

Definition: *Risk Management* is the identification, assessment and prioritization of risks, and the application of resources to minimize, monitor and control the probability and impact of those risks accordingly.

Proficiency Indicators	
For All HR Professionals	**For Advanced HR Professionals**
• Monitors political, economic, social, technological, legal and environmental (PESTLE) factors and their influence on the organization. • Administers and supports HR programs, practices and policies that identify and/or mitigate workplace risk. • Implements crisis management, contingency and business continuity plans for the HR function and the organization. • Communicates critical information about risks (e.g., safety and security) and risk mitigation to employees at all levels. • Conducts due diligence investigations to evaluate risks and ensure legal and regulatory compliance. • Conducts workplace safety- and health-related investigations (e.g., investigates workplace injuries). • Audits risk management activities and plans. • Maintains and ensures accurate reporting of internationally accepted workplace health and safety standards. • Incorporates into business cases the anticipated level of risk.	• Develops, implements and oversees formal and routinized processes for monitoring the organization's internal and external environments, to identify potential risks. • Monitors and evaluates macro-level labor market, industry and global trends for their impact on the organization. • Examines potential threats to the organization and guides senior leadership accordingly. • Develops, implements and oversees a comprehensive enterprise risk management strategy. • Develops crisis management, contingency, and business continuity plans for the HR function and the organization. • Communicates critical information about risks (e.g., safety and security) and risk mitigation to senior-level employees and external stakeholders. • Ensures that risk management activities and plans are audited and that the results inform risk mitigation strategies. • Oversees workplace safety- and health-related investigations and reporting. • Establishes strategies to address workplace retaliation and violence. • Leads after-action debriefs following significant workplace incidents (e.g., those involving employee safety and security). • Evaluates the anticipated level of risk associated with strategic opportunities.

Functional Area #14: Corporate Social Responsibility

Definition: *Corporate Social Responsibility* represents the organization's commitment to operate in an ethical and sustainable manner by engaging in activities that promote and support philanthropy, transparency, sustainability and ethically sound governance practices.

Proficiency Indicators	
For All HR Professionals	**For Advanced HR Professionals**
• Acts as a professional role model and representative of the organization when interacting with the community. • Engages in community-based volunteer and philanthropic activities. • Identifies and promotes opportunities for HR and the organization to engage in corporate social responsibility (CSR) activities. • Helps staff at all levels understand the societal impact of business decisions and the role of the organization's CSR activities in improving the community. • Maintains transparency of HR programs, practices and policies, where appropriate. • Coaches managers to achieve an appropriate level of transparency in organizational practices and decisions. • Identifies opportunities for incorporation of environmentally responsible business practices, and shares them with leadership.	• Serves as a leader in community-based volunteer and philanthropic organizations. • Develops CSR strategies that reflect the organization's mission and values. • Ensures that the organization's CSR programs enhance the employee value proposition and have a beneficial impact on HR programs (e.g., recruitment and retention) and/or contribute to the organization's competitive advantage. • Creates CSR program activities that engage the organization's workforce and the community at large. • Coordinates with other business leaders to integrate CSR objectives throughout the organization. • Coordinates with other business leaders to develop and implement appropriate levels of corporate self-governance and transparency. • Develops, with other business leaders, strategies that encourage and support environmentally responsible business decisions.

Functional Area #15: U.S. Employment Law & Regulations

Definition: *U.S. Employment Law & Regulations* refers to the knowledge and application of all relevant laws and regulations in the United States relating to employment—provisions that set the parameters and limitations for each HR functional area and for organizations overall.

Proficiency Indicators	
For All HR Professionals	**For Advanced HR Professionals**
• Maintains a current working knowledge of relevant domestic and global employment laws. • Ensures that HR programs, practices and policies align and comply with laws and regulations. • Coaches employees at all levels in understanding and avoiding illegal and noncompliant HR-related behaviors (e.g., illegal terminations or discipline, unfair labor practices). • Brokers internal or external legal services for interpretation of employment laws.	• Maintains current, expert knowledge of relevant domestic and global employment laws. • Establishes and monitors criteria for organizational compliance with laws and regulations. • Educates and advises senior leadership on HR-related legal and regulatory compliance issues. • Oversees fulfillment of compliance requirements for HR programs, practices and policies. • Ensures that HR technologies facilitate compliance and reporting requirements (e.g., tracking employee accidents, safety reports).

 **APPENDIX E.**

SHRM Competency Development Plan

Overview

The SHRM Competency Development Plan (CDP) provides an opportunity for every HR professional to pinpoint competency strengths and gaps, then identify activities to leverage those strengths and develop proficiency in competencies in need of improvement. The SHRM CDP is a learning action plan for improving current performance and striving for long-term career goals.

Instructions

For each of the nine competencies included in this plan:

1. Indicate whether you consider the competency a strength or an area of development for you.

2. Indicate the priority group (i.e., how high of a priority is developing this competency for you in your current role).

3. Identify organizational and career goals that align with the competency.

4. Outline activities that align with your organization's goals and your career goals to leverage strengths and develop the competency.

5. Define measures of success, required stakeholder support, potential obstacles and target completion date.

6. Starting with the highest priority group (Priority Group A), select the Annual Conference opportunities that align with the goals you identified.

7. Participate and learn!

Name:_____

Job Title: _____

Career Level:_____

Date:_____

⚖ Ethical Practice

The KSAs needed to maintain high levels of personal and professional integrity, and to act as an ethical agent who promotes core values, integrity, and accountability throughout the organization.

Is this Competency a Strength or Development Area?

Strength	Development Area

Priority Group (select one)

	(A) Important and urgent	(B) Important but not urgent	(C) Less important or optional
	A	B	C

Aligned Organizational Goal(s)

Organizational Goal 1:

Organizational Goal 2:

Organizational Goal 3:

Aligned Career Goal(s)

Career Goal 1:

Career Goal 2:

Career Goal 3:

Activities	Behavioral Indicators / Measures of Success	Stakeholder Support (e.g., coaches, mentors or supporters)	Potential Obstacles	Target Completion Date	Outcome / Notes
Activity 1:					
Activity 2:					
Activity 3:					
Activity 4:					
Activity 5:					

Leadership & Navigation

The KSAs needed to navigate the organization and accomplish HR goals, to create a compelling vision and mission for HR that aligns with the strategic direction and culture of the organization, to lead and promote organizational change, to manage the implementation and execution of HR initiatives, and to promote the role of HR as a key business partner.

Is this Competency a Strength or Development Area?	
Strength	Development Area

Priority Group (select one)			
	(A) Important and urgent	(B) Important but not urgent	(C) Less important or optional
	A	B	C

Aligned Organizational Goal(s)

Organizational Goal 1:

_____

Organizational Goal 2:

_____

Organizational Goal 3:

_____

Aligned Career Goal(s)

Career Goal 1:

_____

Career Goal 2:

_____

Career Goal 3:

_____

Activities	Behavioral Indicators / Measures of Success	Stakeholder Support (e.g., coaches, mentors or supporters)	Potential Obstacles	Target Completion Date	Outcome / Notes
Activity 1:					
Activity 2:					
Activity 3:					
Activity 4:					
Activity 5:					

Business Acumen

The KSAs needed to understand the organization's operations, functions, and external environment, and to apply business tools and analyses that inform HR initiatives and operations consistent with the overall strategic direction of the organization.

Is this Competency a Strength or Development Area?	
Strength	Development Area

Priority Group (select one)			
	(A) Important and urgent	**(B) Important but not urgent**	**(C) Less important or optional**
	A	B	C

Aligned Organizational Goal(s)

Organizational Goal 1:

Organizational Goal 2:

Organizational Goal 3:

Aligned Career Goal(s)

Career Goal 1:

Career Goal 2:

Career Goal 3:

Activities	Behavioral Indicators / Measures of Success	Stakeholder Support (e.g., coaches, mentors or supporters)	Potential Obstacles	Target Completion Date	Outcome / Notes
Activity 1:					
Activity 2:					
Activity 3:					
Activity 4:					
Activity 5:					

Consultation

The KSAs needed to work with organizational stakeholders in evaluating business challenges and identifying opportunities for the design, implementation, and evaluation of change initiatives, and to build ongoing support for HR solutions that meet the changing needs of customers and the business.

Is this Competency a Strength or Development Area?	
Strength	Development Area

Priority Group (select one)			
	(A) Important and urgent	(B) Important but not urgent	(C) Less important or optional
	A	B	C

Aligned Organizational Goal(s)

Organizational Goal 1:

_____

Organizational Goal 2:

_____

Organizational Goal 3:

_____

Aligned Career Goal(s)

Career Goal 1:

_____

Career Goal 2:

_____

Career Goal 3:

_____

Activities	Behavioral Indicators / Measures of Success	Stakeholder Support (e.g., coaches, mentors or supporters)	Potential Obstacles	Target Completion Date	Outcome / Notes
Activity 1:					
Activity 2:					
Activity 3:					
Activity 4:					
Activity 5:					

Critical Evaluation

The KSAs needed to collect and analyze qualitative and quantitative data, and to interpret and promote findings that evaluate HR initiatives and inform business decisions and recommendations.

Is this Competency a Strength or Development Area?	
Strength	Development Area

Priority Group (select one)			
	(A) Important and urgent	(B) Important but not urgent	(C) Less important or optional
	A	B	C

Aligned Organizational Goal(s)

Organizational Goal 1:

_____

Organizational Goal 2:

_____

Organizational Goal 3:

Aligned Career Goal(s)

Career Goal 1:

_____

Career Goal 2:

_____

Career Goal 3:

_____

Activities	Behavioral Indicators / Measures of Success	Stakeholder Support (e.g., coaches, mentors or supporters)	Potential Obstacles	Target Completion Date	Outcome / Notes
Activity 1:					
Activity 2:					
Activity 3:					
Activity 4:					
Activity 5:					

Communication

The KSAs needed to effectively craft and deliver concise and informative communications, to listen to and address the concerns of others, and to transfer and translate information from one level or unit of the organization to another.

Is this Competency a Strength or Development Area?	
Strength	Development Area

Priority Group (select one)			
	(A) Important and urgent	(B) Important but not urgent	(C) Less important or optional
	A	B	C

Aligned Organizational Goal(s)

Organizational Goal 1:

Organizational Goal 2:

Organizational Goal 3:

Aligned Career Goal(s)

Career Goal 1:

Career Goal 2:

Career Goal 3:

Activities	Behavioral Indicators / Measures of Success	Stakeholder Support (e.g., coaches, mentors or supporters)	Potential Obstacles	Target Completion Date	Outcome / Notes
Activity 1:					
Activity 2:					
Activity 3:					
Activity 4:					
Activity 5:					

Global & Cultural Effectiveness

The KSAs needed to value and consider the perspectives and backgrounds of all parties, to interact with others in a global context, and to promote a diverse and inclusive workplace.

Is this Competency a Strength or Development Area?	
Strength	Development Area

Priority Group (select one)			
	(A) Important and urgent	(B) Important but not urgent	(C) Less important or optional
	A	B	C

Aligned Organizational Goal(s)

Organizational Goal 1:

_____

Organizational Goal 2:

_____

Organizational Goal 3:

_____

Aligned Career Goal(s)

Career Goal 1:

_____

Career Goal 2:

_____

Career Goal 3:

_____

Activities	Behavioral Indicators / Measures of Success	Stakeholder Support (e.g., coaches, mentors or supporters)	Potential Obstacles	Target Completion Date	Outcome / Notes
Activity 1:					
Activity 2:					
Activity 3:					
Activity 4:					
Activity 5:					

Relationship Management

The KSAs needed to create and maintain a network of professional contacts within and outside of the organization, to build and maintain relationships, to work as an effective member of a team, and to manage conflict while supporting the organization.

Is this Competency a Strength or Development Area?	
Strength	Development Area

Priority Group (select one)			
	(A) Important and urgent	(B) Important but not urgent	(C) Less important or optional
	A	B	C

Aligned Organizational Goal(s)

Organizational Goal 1:

Organizational Goal 2:

Organizational Goal 3:

Aligned Career Goal(s)

Career Goal 1:

Career Goal 2:

Career Goal 3:

Activities	Behavioral Indicators / Measures of Success	Stakeholder Support (e.g., coaches, mentors or supporters)	Potential Obstacles	Target Completion Date	Outcome / Notes
Activity 1:					
Activity 2:					
Activity 3:					
Activity 4:					
Activity 5:					

HR Expertise
The knowledge of principles, practices, and functions of effective human resource management.

Is this Competency a Strength or Development Area?		
Strength	Development Area	

Priority Group (select one)			
	(A) Important and urgent	(B) Important but not urgent	(C) Less important or optional
	A	B	C

Aligned Organizational Goal(s)

Organizational Goal 1:

Organizational Goal 2:

Organizational Goal 3:

Aligned Career Goal(s)

Career Goal 1:

Career Goal 2:

Career Goal 3:

Activities	Behavioral Indicators / Measures of Success	Stakeholder Support (e.g., coaches, mentors or supporters)	Potential Obstacles	Target Completion Date	Outcome / Notes
Activity 1:					
Activity 2:					
Activity 3:					
Activity 4:					
Activity 5:					

Endnotes and References

Introduction

[1] Society for Human Resource Management, SHRM 2016 Trends Report (Alexandria, VA: SHRM, 2016).

Chapter 1

[1] U.S. Army Heritage and Education Center, "Who First Originated the Term VUCA (Volatility, Uncertainty, Complexity and Ambiguity)?," http://usawc.libanswers.com/faq/84869

[2] Society for Human Resource Management, *SHRM Competency Model* (Alexandria, VA: SHRM, 2017), www.shrm.org/LearningAndCareer/competency-model/PublishingImages/pages/default/SHRM%20Competency%20Model_Detailed%20Report_Final_SECURED.pdf

Chapter 2

[1] David C. McClelland, "Testing for Competence Rather Than 'Intelligence,'" *American Psychologist* 28, no. 1 (January 1973): 1-14.

[2] Farhan Kalid, Role of the HR Business Partner, The Ins and Outs of HR Management, http://www.hrminsider.com/role-of-hr-business-partner

[3] Society for Human Resource Management, *SHRM Competency Model* (Alexandria, VA: SHRM, 2017), www.shrm.org/LearningAndCareer/competency-model/PublishingImages/pages/default/SHRM%20Competency%20Model_Detailed%20Report_Final_SECURED.pdf

[4] Ibid.

[5] Ibid.

[6] Ibid.

Chapter 3

[1] Society for Human Resource Management, 2017 SHRM Learning System, SHRM, 2017, https://www.shrm.org/certification/learning/Pages/default. aspx?gclid=CMGgj8WH3tICFQSRfgod-AEJWQ

Part III

[1] 2017 SHRM Learning System, SHRM, 2017, https://www.shrm.org/certification/ learning/Pages/default.aspx?gclid=CMGgj8WH3tICFQSRfgod-AEJWQ

Chapter 10

[1] Society for Human Resource Management, *SHRM Competency Model* (Alexandria, VA: SHRM, 2017), www.shrm.org/LearningAndCareer/competency-model/ PublishingImages/pages/default/SHRM%20Competency%20Model_Detailed%20 Report_Final_SECURED.pdf

Appendix B

[1] Cause-Driven Leadership, Competency Development Guide, YMCA USA, 2013

Appendix C

[1] SHRM Interactive Competency Model: https://www.shrm.org/learningandcareer/ competency-model/pages/default.aspx

Appendix D

[1] Proficiency Indicators, SHRM BoCK, SHRM 2017. Download the entire SHRM BoCK at https://www.shrm.org/certification/Documents/SHRM-BoCK-FINAL. pdf

Appendix E

[1] SHRM Competency Development Plan, SHRM 2017

About the Author

Phyllis G. Hartman, SPHR, is the founder of PGHR Consulting, Inc., and has spent close to 30 years as an HR professional. A frequent speaker on HR, business, and career development topics, Hartman is a member of SHRM's Ethics and Corporate Social Responsibility and Sustainability Special Expertise Panel. She is also an active member of the SHRM Advocacy Team (A-Team), providing advocacy for HR legislation. She has done volunteer work for the SHRM Foundation and has participated on various task groups for SHRM.

This is Hartman's third book. She co-authored *Never Get Lost Again: Navigating Your HR Career* with Nancy Glube in 2009 and wrote *Looking to Hire an HR Leader?* in 2014. She has written articles, white papers, and book chapters on HR topics, and she teaches human resources and business courses at several Pittsburgh colleges and universities.

She was the recipient of a Distinguished Alumni Award in 2013 from La Roche College, where she was a visiting professor and temporary HR department chair in 2015-16. She has delivered programs at the SHRM Annual Conference, as well as at the Pennsylvania, Utah, Vermont, and Virginia SHRM State Councils, SHRM Student Conferences, and local SHRM and business organizations. She has held leadership positions in the Pennsylvania SHRM State Council and the Pittsburgh HR Association.

Hartman is a member of the Executive Service Corps of the Bayer Center for Nonprofit Management and does volunteer teaching and consulting for not-for-profits in the Pittsburgh area. She is also a volunteer for the Ward Home, an organization that provides support for foster children.

In her business, she has provided a variety of HR consulting services to small- and mid-sized organizations. Prior to founding PGHR, she worked as a practitioner in HR management in for-profit manufacturing and nonprofit service sectors.

Hartman holds a master's in human resource management from La Roche College and a bachelor's in education from Edinboro University of Pennsylvania. She holds the SHRM-SCP credential.

Hartman lives outside of Pittsburgh with her husband, Chuck. She enjoys spending time with her son, Matt, daughter-in-law, Emma, and granddaughter, Penelope. She is an active hiker, an amateur yogini, a birdwatcher, a puzzle-solver, and a reader.

Index

Page numbers appended with an italic *f, t,* or *w* indicate figures, tables, or worksheets.

Consultation competency, 52, 100–101*t*

Critical Evaluation competency, 55, 102–3*t*

Ethical Practice competency, 57, 90–91*t*

Global and Cultural Effectiveness competency, 44, 96–97*t*

Leadership and Navigation competency, 59, 88–89*t*

Relationship Management competency, 46, 92–93*t*

succession development and planning, 84

Sukenik, Phil, 83

supervisors/managers

competency assessment input from, 29

HR competencies for managing and developing others, 67–68, 67*t,* 68–69*t*

T

Talent Acquisition (HR functional area), 22, 104*t*

talent management/employee development subcompetency, 67–68, 68–69*t*

technical competencies, 10, 61, 61–63*t*

technological change and HR competencies, 5–7

Technology Management (HR functional area), 24, 110*t*

time limitations, 82

Total Rewards (HR functional area), 23, 106*t*

U

Ulrich, David, 9

U.S. Employment Law & Regulations (HR functional area), 25–26, 114*t*

V

vision subcompetency, 59, 88*t*

volatile, uncertain, complex, and ambiguous (VUCA) business world, 5–7

W

Wade, Sally, 83

Widger, Beverly, 83

Workforce Management (HR functional area), 23–24, 108*t*

Workplace Group of HR functions, 24–26

Additional
SHRM-Published Books

View from the Top: Leveraging Human and Organization Capital to Create Value
Richard L. Antoine, Libby Sartain, Dave Ulrich, Patrick M. Wright

California Employment Law: An Employer's Guide, Revised & Updated for 2017
James J. McDonald, Jr.

101 Sample Write-ups for Documenting Employee Performance Problems: A Guide to Progressive Discipline & Termination, Third Edition
Paul Falcone

Developing Business Acumen
SHRM Competency Series:
Making an Impact in Small Business
Jennifer Currence

Applying Critical Evaluation
SHRM Competency Series:
Making an Impact in Small Business
Jennifer Currence

Touching People's Lives:
Leaders' Sorrow or Joy
Michael R. Losey

From Hello to Goodbye:
Proactive Tips for Maintaining Positive Employee Relations, Second Edition
Christine V. Walters

Defining HR Success:
9 Critical Competencies for HR Professionals
Kari R. Strobel, James N. Kurtessis, Debra J. Cohen, and Alexander Alonso

HR on Purpose:
Developing Deliberate People Passion
Steve Browne

A Manager's Guide to Developing Competencies in HR Staff
Phyllis G. Hartman

Tips and Tools for Improving Proficiency in Your Reports
Phyllis G. Hartman

Developing Proficiency in HR:
7 Self-Directed Activities for HR Professionals
Debra J. Cohen

Manager Onboarding:
5 Steps for Setting New Leaders Up for Success
Sharlyn Lauby

Destination Innovation:
HR's Role in Charting the Course
Patricia M. Buhler

Got a Solution? HR Approaches to 5 Common and Persistent Business Problems
Dale J. Dwyer & Sheri A. Caldwell

HR's Greatest Challenge: Driving the C-Suite to Improve Employee Engagement and Retention
Richard P. Finnegan

Business-Focused HR:
11 Processes to Drive Results
Shane S. Douthitt & Scott P. Mondore

Proving the Value of HR: How and Why to Measure ROI, Second Edition
Jack J. Phillips & Patricia Pulliam Phillips

SHRMStore Books Approved for Recertification Credit

Aligning HR & Business Strategy/Holbeche, 9780750680172 (2009)

Becoming the Evidence-Based Manager/Latham, 9780891063988 (2009)

Being Global/Cabrera, 9781422183229 (2012)

Best Practices in Succession Planning/Linkage, 9780787985790 (2007)

Calculating Success/Hoffmann, 9781422166390 (2012)

Collaborate/Sanker, 9781118114728 (2012)

Deep Dive/Horwath, 9781929774821 (2009)

Effective HR Management/Lawler, 9780804776875 (2012)

Emotional Intelligence/Bradbury, 9780974320625 (2009)

Employee Engagement/Carbonara, 9780071799508 (2012)

From Hello to Goodbye/Walters, 9781586442064 (2011)

Handbook for Strategic HR/Vogelsang, 9780814432495 (2012)

Hidden Drivers of Success/Schiemann, 9781586443337 (2013)

HR at Your Service/Latham, 9781586442477 (2012)

HR Transformation/Ulrich, 9780071638708 (2009)

Lean HR/Lay, 9781481914208 (2013)

Manager 3.0/Karsh, 97808144w32891 (2013)

Managing Employee Turnover/Allen, 9781606493403 (2012)

Managing the Global Workforce/Caliguri, 9781405107327 (2010)

Managing the Mobile Workforce/Clemons, 9780071742207 (2010)

Managing Older Workers/Cappelli, 9781422131657 (2010)

Multipliers/Wiseman, 9780061964398 (2010)

Negotiation at Work/Asherman, 9780814431900 (2012)

Nine Minutes on Monday/Robbins, 9780071801980 (2012)

SHRMStore Books Approved for Recertification Credit continued

One Strategy/Sinofsky, 9780470560457 (2009)

People Analytics/Waber, 9780133158311 (2013)

Performance Appraisal Tool Kit/Falcone, 9780814432631 (2013)

Point Counterpoint/Tavis, 9781586442767 (2012)

Practices for Engaging the 21st Century Workforce/Castellano, 9780133086379 (2013)

Proving the Value of HR/Phillips, 9781586442880 (2012)

Reality-Based Leadership/Wakeman, 9780470613504 (2010)

Social Media Strategies/Golden, 9780470633106 (2010)

Talent, Transformations, and Triple Bottom Line/Savitz, 9781118140970 (2013)

The Big Book of HR/Mitchell, 9781601631893 (2012)

The Crowdsourced Performance Review/Mosley, 9780071817981 (2013)

The Definitive Guide to HR Communications/Davis, 9780137061433 (2011)

The e-HR Advantage/Waddill, 9781904838340 (2011)

The Employee Engagement Mindset/Clark, 9780071788298 (2012)

The Global Challenge/Evans, 9780073530376 (2010)

The Global Tango/Trompenaars, 9780071761154 (2010)

The HR Answer Book/Smith, 9780814417171 (2011)

The Manager's Guide to HR/Muller, 9780814433027 (2013)

The Power of Appreciative Inquiry/Whitney, 9781605093284 (2010)

Transformative HR/Boudreau, 9781118036044 (2011)

What If? Short Stories to Spark Diversity Dialogue/Robbins, 9780891062752 (2008)

What Is Global Leadership?/Gundling, 9781904838234 (2011)

Winning the War for Talent/Johnson, 9780730311553 (2011)